Francine Jay is the author of the international bestseller *The Joy of Less* and founder of MissMinimalist.com. She has helped hundreds of thousands of people organize their homes and simplify their lives, and has been prominently featured in international media, including the *New York Times*, the BBC, the *Guardian*, CNN, the *Financial Times* and the Huffington Post. She lives in Portland, Oregon with her husband and daughter.

lightly

HOW TO LIVE
A SIMPLE, SERENE
& STRESS - FREE LIFE

FRANCINE JAY

Quercus

First published in Great Britain in 2019 by

Quercus Editions Ltd
Carmelite House
50 Victoria Embankment
London EC4Y 0DZ

An Hachette UK company

A CIP catalogue record for this book is available from the British Library

ISBN 978 1 52940 081 6
EBOOK ISBN 978 1 52940 080 9

10 9 8 7 6 5 4 3 2 1

Illustrations and hand-lettering © 2019 Ryn Frank

Book design © Melissa Lofty

"Along a mountain path" by Matsuo Basho translated by William R. Nelson and Takafumi Saito from 1020 Haiku in Translation: The Heart of Basho, Buson and Issa. English translation copyright © 2006 by Takafumi Saito and William R. Nelson. Reprinted by permission of William R. Nelson.

Excerpts from "The Adventure of a Skier" translated by Ann Goldstein from Difficult Loves by Italo Calvino. Text copyright © 1958 by Giulio Einaudi Editore, S.p.A. Torino. English translation © 2017 by Ann Goldstein. Reprinted by permission of the Wylie Agency. All rights reserved.

Printed and bound in Italy by L.E.G.O. S.p.A.

for

JULIET

contents

lighten your step

lighten your stress

lighten your spirit

introduction

Do you ever feel like life is weighing you down? Like the stuff in your home, the to-dos in your schedule, the worries in your heart are too much?

As we go about our days, life can get heavy. We don't set out to burden ourselves, but we're naturally inclined to accumulate things—possessions, responsibilities, emotions—rather than release them. And when we're trying to keep up with work, family, and other commitments, we don't even notice the inflow. Before we know it, our closets are overstuffed, our calendars are overbooked, and our spirits are overwhelmed.

But here's the good news: It doesn't have to be that way. If we want, we can shake off many of those burdens and live more lightly. We can breeze through our days rather than drag through them. In this book, I'll show you how.

First, let me tell you why I became a minimalist: I fell in love with traveling lightly. After a few trips lugging around a heavy suitcase, I vowed henceforth to travel with just a small carry-on.

The experience was liberating! Without the excess baggage, I felt free as a bird—energetic, unencumbered, and ready for anything.

I wanted to re-create this same feeling of freedom in my everyday life. So in between trips, I cleared the excess from my household. Every bag of discards felt like a weight lifted from my shoulders.

"Lightly" became my mantra. It started with the stuff in my home but grew to encompass my entire life. Whether I was facing an excess of cookware, commitments, or anxieties, I'd ask myself: How can I cast off some of this weight?

As I pared down, my spirits soared. Stress and fatigue fell away. I began to move through my days with more ease, efficiency, and grace.

"Lightly" transformed my life, and it can transform yours, too.

This book is a minimalist manual for everyone—whether you want to strip down your stuff to the essentials or simply free some space in your coat closet. Whether you want to overhaul your schedule or just gain an hour or two in the evening. Whether you want to change your entire outlook on life or just get rid of a nagging guilt.

You can lighten up a little or a lot. How far you take it is entirely up to you. In these pages, I'll give you all the techniques, the philosophy, and the inspiration you need. They'll be here for you whenever you're ready.

There's no shortage of decluttering books on the market—

perhaps you've read a few yourself. Maybe the methods didn't work for you; or they did, but the clutter has started to creep back in. Maybe you purged your excess and organized the rest, but haven't achieved the satisfaction and serenity you expected. Perhaps you're wondering, "What's the point?" or "What's next?"

Lightly is different: It goes beyond decluttering—far beyond—to uplift your thoughts, your actions, every moment and aspect of your life. When you declutter and call it a day, it's easy to backslide. But when your entire life is aligned to a guiding principle—*to live lightly*—you'll find a new sense of purpose and fulfillment, and a powerful incentive to stay on the path.

The best part: There's no pressure. You don't have to follow a program, do everything in order, or do it all at once. I've written this book so you can pick it up anytime, turn to any page, and be inspired.

The first section, Lighten Your Stuff, shows you exactly how to slim down the contents of your home. Simplifying your surroundings is the first step toward living more lightly; an open, airy space calms your soul and lifts your spirit.

Possessions can be powerful psychological triggers; it's almost as if emotions get stuck to your stuff. When you release physical clutter, mental clutter often gets swept away with it, giving you a jump start on your path to inner well-being.

Lightening up your stuff doesn't have to be tedious or complicated. I've distilled the process to a few powerful techniques that make it easy and enjoyable. Whether you're tackling one drawer or an entire room, they make light work of letting go.

Which brings me to an important point: Feel free to start small and go slowly. Most of us don't have the time or energy to clear out our entire homes in one fell swoop. Instead, we do our decluttering in fits and starts when we have a free hour or two.

That's why I've devoted separate sections to each category of stuff. Think of it like a recipe book for minimalism: Whatever you're reducing, from books to bags to shoes to sheets, you can turn to the relevant page for advice and inspiration. No need to read through an entire chapter when you're just wondering how to pare down your plates.

And you don't have to follow the sections in order. Start with stuff that's easy for you, and work your way up to bigger challenges. If you have no strong attachment to your office supplies or kitchen gadgets, work on those first. When you see how good it feels to let go, you'll build the confidence and momentum to address your beloved books or family heirlooms.

The general techniques, plus category-specific advice, are all you need to eliminate the excess. Go for it! I'll be right here to hold your hand and help you through it.

I start with curating your home simply because it's the natural entry point to a lighter lifestyle. It's hard to focus on more abstract burdens, like your commitments and worries, when you're surrounded by clutter. It's also easier to develop non-attachment to superficial things (like your socks) before diving into the deeper waters of your mind and spirit. But if you've already tidied up,

To enjoy life,
we must touch
much of it
LIGHTLY.

VOLTAIRE

feel free to leap right in to later sections; you can always come back to the Stuff chapter if you need a refresher.

So here's the exciting part: Minimalism doesn't end with spacious closets and emptier drawers. Lightening your stuff has an amazing ripple effect on other areas of your life.

As you clear out your excess, you'll become significantly more mindful of your impact on the planet. Lighten Your Step shows you a number of ways, both big and small, to reduce it. The more lightly we live on the earth, the cleaner, healthier, and more beautiful it will be for present and future generations.

Dealing with stuff is just half the equation; our schedules need curating, too. Lighten Your Stress helps you set priorities and put systems in place so you can lead a less-busy life. The goal is not to get more done, but to have less to do. Fewer distractions and more focus lead to freer, more fulfilling days.

And let's not forget about inner clutter. Worries, drama, and emotional baggage can weigh us down just as much as possessions can. Lighten Your Spirit helps you let go of negative thoughts, feelings, and other stressors to free up your heart and mind for deeper, happier, more meaningful experiences. You may even feel a new interconnectedness and harmony with the world around you. How wonderful does that sound?

I'm also excited to share with you some of my favorite quotes and sources of inspiration—think of them as invitations to further exploration. If Scandinavian design, Stoic philosophy, or the *Yoga Sutras* speak to you, listen to and follow your heart. There are many paths to a lighter, more meaningful life, and I'd love to help you find yours.

Lightly is a concise and coherent philosophy of life. Instead of cobbling together guidance from a variety of books — then struggling to recall it in those moments you need it most — all you have to remember is one word. It doesn't get any easier than that.

Lightly is also a powerful filter for making decisions. Whether you're tempted by an impulse purchase, trying to resist a chocolate donut, or struggling to say no to another obligation, simply think "Lightly" to know how to proceed. Instead of weighing pros and cons in each situation, you'll have a single touchstone to help you live your values.

My hope is that you'll keep this book close — on your coffee table, in your carryall — and dip into it anytime for a moment of inspiration or a practical tip for a current problem. It's designed so you can come back to it, over months, years, or decades, to find guidance for any situation or stage of life. Circumstances are always changing; a new home, baby, job, or relationship can upend the most perfectly curated life. Whether you're suddenly faced with an influx of possessions, expectations, or difficult emotions, you can flip to a page in Lightly for the help you need.

Make "Lightly" your mantra, one lovely little word to live by. With each page of this book, you'll jettison more weight; and before long, you'll be floating through life with a new lightness of being.

lighten your
stuff

Let go of your excess possessions and you'll instantly feel lighter. In this section, I'll show you how to curate your stuff to perfectly match your needs. You'll find general techniques followed by specific advice for everything you own. Feel free to skip around and come back as you're ready to tackle your clothes, kitchen items, or office supplies. Have fun choosing your favorite things!

techniques

let it go {
CLEAN SLATE
CONSOLIDATE
CURATE
}

put it here {
OUT BOX
ON HOLD
ORGANIZE
}

keep it light {
REFINE
REIGN
RESTRAINT
}

clean slate

If you've ever tried to declutter, you know how tedious it can be to pick through a drawer, closet, or cabinet, looking for things to get rid of. You're likely to let many things slide and leave them where they are, just to be done with the chore.

There's an easier, more effective way to lighten your stuff: Start with a Clean Slate. In other words, take that drawer, closet, cabinet, or other area of excess and completely empty its contents. Dump it out, clear it off, strip it bare of everything.

With almost zero effort, you have a beautiful, empty space. How's that for instant gratification? Now it's more expedient to get rid of the stuff than to put it back. In order to keep something, you'll have to justify why it belongs there and then physically return it to the space. That's harder than just sweeping it into a bag and letting it go.

That's why a Clean Slate is so magical: It lets you bypass decluttering altogether and get straight to the business of curating your stuff. It's about deciding what to keep, rather than what to toss.

It sounds like the opposite of tidying up, but trust me on this one. Sometimes you need to make a mess on your way to a more serene space. If you don't pull everything out, the results won't be nearly as thorough or dramatic.

A Clean Slate leaves nowhere for stuff to hide. Do you have any idea what's lurking in the back of your coat closet or the darkest recesses of your kitchen cabinets? If you don't completely empty them, you never will. Stuff that's tucked away is out of sight and out of mind. It can hide away indefinitely, escaping traditional decluttering techniques. A Clean Slate flushes them out and addresses them once and for all.

A Clean Slate also overcomes inertia—sometimes the only force holding your clutter in place. Do you have stuff in your household that hasn't moved in months, years, or (gasp) decades? Just because you can't remember life without it doesn't mean you should keep it.

Once you've emptied things out, take a few minutes and gaze at that glorious space. Picture how lovely it'll be—no longer stuffed to the gills but holding a well-edited collection of your favorite things. With any luck, you'll find yourself pretty reluctant to put the mess back in.

And sometimes, something quite wondrous happens: You return so few items to a storage space, you don't even need it anymore. It's exhilarating to purge dressers, file cabinets, and plastic storage bins right along with their contents. If you clear out a larger space—like a closet, spare room, basement, or garage—you can even repurpose it for a favorite activity.

A Clean Slate leaves you with an empty space, a pile of stuff, and a magnificent sense of possibility. Are you starting to feel lighter already? All you need to do is decide what adds value to your life, pluck it from the pile, and send the remainder on its way. The less you save, the more quickly you'll be done!

consolidate

When deciding what to keep, consolidate like-with-like items. Why is this so important? Because it's a lot easier to let things go when you have a million others just like it.

Make a pile of plates, pens, pillowcases, or whatever it is you're working on. Seeing them all together can be an illuminating experience and a powerful incentive to lighten things up.

Search your household to find all the multiples. These duplicates often go their separate ways and end up in different parts of the house. If you've stashed some office supplies in your bedroom or sweaters in your spouse's closet, round up all of them before you proceed.

Once you've consolidated a category of items, count them. You may be shocked at how many you have. And while you might make a good case for owning one, three, or even a half dozen of something, you'll be hard-pressed to justify a double-digit figure.

Consolidation is a little bit of tough love, as it puts you face-to-face with your excess. You can be in denial (or completely unaware) of this surfeit when it's spread throughout the house. It's that incredulous "I really have twenty-five pairs of shoes?" moment that spurs you into action.

You might be mystified at how you acquired such a collection. Here's how it happens: We often don't throw away our old things when we replace them with better ones. "They're still good" and "we might need them someday," so the pile grows and grows. We usually don't even notice until we run out of places to put them.

In some cases, we're not sure what the items are for, or what they belong to (like those mysterious cables, chargers, and flat-pack furniture parts). Others simply defy explanation: We just seem drawn to accumulate T-shirts, yoga pants, cookbooks, cosmetics, or some other random item.

Consolidation is so powerful because it pinpoints these trouble spots, showing you exactly where you can lighten up. You don't have to wander your house thinking, "What's weighing me down?" The answer is loud and clear.

But take heart. Such plenitude makes it a cinch to pare down. When you've counted thirty-two coffee mugs, you can purge half of them with no problem. Instead of agonizing over their departure, you can feel grateful for your abundance and rest easy with the knowledge that you'll still have plenty.

After you've cleared out the excess, keep the remainder consolidated. That way, you can nip clutter in the bud if your supply starts growing again. Your things will also be easier to find when you need them. You'll no longer have to search your entire house for a "lost" item or buy a second of something you already have. That means less stress, less expense, and less stuff down the road.

curate

After you've consolidated like-with-like, it's time for the fun part of lightening up: choosing what to keep.

How to determine what makes the cut? It's simple: *Keep only those items that make your life easier or happier.* Enjoy the process of selecting your favorite things. It gives you a chance to admire and appreciate the lovely stuff you have.

What if they all seem like favorites? Well, according to the Pareto Principle, we use 20 percent of our stuff 80 percent of the time. That means that the vast majority of our possessions are *not* that special or important, and our lives would go on just as well without them. Curating is identifying that magical 20 percent and decluttering much of the rest.

Curating takes the idea of a capsule wardrobe — a small collection of ultra-versatile clothing to suit all occasions — and expands it to your entire household. The goal: to have a well-edited set of possessions that's perfectly in sync with your needs.

In fact, after you curate your stuff, you'll be amazed at how effortless your daily routine becomes. With the excess out of the way, you avoid the decision fatigue that comes with too many choices. Instead of wasting time and energy on trivial matters (Which shirt matches these pants? Which coffee cup should I use?), you'll move through your days more smoothly and efficiently.

Of course, with any project, the toughest part is getting

started. My advice: Start with the stuff you don't use or don't like. (It's really that easy!)

You may be surprised to realize how much of your stuff you don't even *want*. Be honest with yourself about those gifts, heirlooms, and shopping mistakes, like the musty "antiques" you inherited, the kitschy socks your brother gave you, or the shoes you splurged on but never wear. Are you keeping them out of a sense of guilt or obligation?

You have permission to get rid of them. Life is too short to live with things you don't like.

Next, move on to multiples: Save only your favorites or a reasonable amount. Be selective — you deserve to use your best things on a daily basis. When we have duplicates, we often use our old, shabby things and save the better ones for "special occasions." Ditch the duplicates, and use your good stuff now.

Think of it this way: If you had space for only one of each item, which would you keep? It's like packing a suitcase with your best-loved things.

Remember, space is just as important as stuff. You don't have to fill every drawer, closet, or room just because you can. In fact, you'll feel a lot better if you have some breathing space.

In my home, I love to use the design concept of "white space" — that is, having some emptiness around objects rather than crowding them. White space not only creates visual calm and serenity, it highlights the important items in our lives.

Even better, white space makes room for activity — for you to do yoga, your spouse to host poker night, or your preschooler to practice her ballet moves. Your home is living space, not storage space. It should reflect what you do, rather than what you own.

As you evaluate your stuff, consider the story it tells. Our possessions reveal much about our hopes and fears, ambitions and dreams, past and present. We don't want them airing our unrealized goals, unfinished projects, or unsuccessful relationships. Living with such reminders can be a huge psychological burden, holding us down and tethering us to the past.

Curating is a marvelous opportunity for self-reflection, and makes us ask questions that go beyond our possessions. In the process, we make peace with our past (ditch that gift from an ex), embrace our present (keep the jeans that fit now), and shape our future (toss books from a former career).

When you curate, cast off anything and everything with negative associations and surround yourself only with bits of happiness. Make sure your things tell the story of the life you *want* to live.

out box

It may sound surprising, but a humble little cardboard box can be your most powerful tool in living more lightly. Let me explain . . .

Stuff flows into our homes with ease. Nary a day goes by without a new object making an entrance—whether it comes in a shopping bag, through the mail slot, or via our children's backpacks.

The problem: It's easy for stuff to get in, but far more difficult to get it out. Once they've made it inside, things become comfortably ensconced in our households. Even when we *want* to get rid of something, we're often at a loss for *how*.

Think about it: How many times have you come across an item you no longer need, but had no idea what to do with it? You likely returned it to the drawer and figured you'd deal with it later (during your next charity shop run or "official" decluttering session).

That's why every home needs an Out Box. It's an exit route for unwanted stuff. Your Out Box can be as simple as a large cardboard box tucked in your coat closet, laundry room, or other convenient spot. Whenever you (or family members) come across something to discard, simply put it in the box. Dealing with your excess couldn't be easier.

If you want to get fancy—or entice your spouse or children to use it—cover it with colored paper or write a cheeky label (like "Stuff We Don't Need," "Let It Go," or "Lightly"). Give it a little flair, and it'll attract some interest and clearly convey its purpose. Your Out Box should give off positive decluttering vibes, reminding you and your family that it's good to get rid of stuff you don't need.

We often put off purging our stuff because we think we have to dedicate an entire day or weekend to the task. Some popular decluttering programs recommend we do it all at once, but I don't think that's necessary or particularly doable.

You don't have to save decluttering for a special day. In fact, it's far more effective to make it a lifestyle. That's what's so wonderful about an Out Box: It helps you lighten up, little by little, on a daily basis.

When you pull a duplicate potato peeler out of your kitchen drawer, put it in your Out Box. When you put on then take off that unflattering blouse, put it in your Out Box. When you finish that novel you'll never read again, put it in your Out Box. When you come across anything that's outgrown, unused, or unloved, put it in your Out Box.

Your Out Box removes unneeded items from your daily life, providing a space for them before they leave. It consolidates your castoffs so you can deal with them all at once—donating, selling, or otherwise disposing of them when you have the time. For all intents and purposes, they're "gone" and simply awaiting transport to their new home.

Furthermore, the Out Box has a built-in fail-safe: The delay between putting an item in the box and donating its contents leaves a comfortable margin for error. We're often afraid that if we toss something, we'll need it the very next day (and be racked with regret for discarding it). An Out Box alleviates these worries. That item will still be there the next day and likely quite a few days after that. In fact, the longer it sits there, the more we realize we really don't need it.

Take joy in filling your Out Box! You're not only lightening your load, you're sharing your excess with someone in need. You're recognizing that you have enough and can spread that abundance in your community. You're keeping perfectly good items out of a landfill and giving them another chance to be loved. You're doing good with your decluttering.

So fill it up, donate the contents, and fill it up again. Make your Out Box a permanent fixture, and add something new to it each and every day. The heavier your box becomes, the lighter your home.

on hold

As we lift the weight from our lives, some difficult items might slow us down. They're not essentials, but for some reason or other, we're not quite ready to show them the exit.

This is where many of us lose confidence and momentum and decide we'll never be minimalists after all. But here's a technique to glide right over this trouble spot and keep on going: Put those items On Hold.

On Hold is one of my best-kept secrets to lightening up. Why a secret? Because hiding something away, even temporarily, doesn't seem very minimalist.

I resisted this technique for years for that very reason. Here's what turned me around: After I had a child, I realized the complexities of decluttering a little one's things. More specifically, that they're likely to ask for something immediately after you get rid of it, and no amount of logic or reasoning ("you're much too big for that push toy") will help.

So to avoid the tantrums, distress, and fear of turning my daughter into a hoarder, I started putting her outgrown things On Hold. I'd simply stash them away in a hidden bin for six months. If they weren't requested during that time period, they were safe to send elsewhere. Potential discards were out of sight, but easily retrievable if she suddenly became nostalgic for old playthings.

This method worked so well for her that I started (secretly) using it myself. And while I thought I was backsliding, putting my stuff On Hold actually took my decluttering to the next level.

Yes, even a minimalist can have trouble saying farewell to something. When faced with a problematic item, I find putting it On Hold the best option. It's the first step toward making a psychological break with it. Simply marking it for removal makes it suddenly less special, and the balance of power shifts. In (remarkably little) time, the item loses its grip on me, and I'm ready to let it go. Using this method, I've been able to release items I've wrestled with for years in just a few months.

Is On Hold a bit of a crutch? Maybe, but it works. I think of it more as physical therapy. It helps you develop those minimalist muscles and avoid the paralysis brought on by more challenging items. It's a gentler way to ease something out of your life.

Putting something On Hold feels comfortable, because you know you can retrieve it if you have regrets. But amazingly enough, I've never reclaimed anything On Hold, and you probably won't either.

Once those items are packed away, they somehow lose their magic. Seeing them as potential discards, rather than lifelong possessions, breaks the spell they have over you. On Hold helps you realize you can live without them after all.

So don't worry if you can't add something directly to your Out Box. Sometimes a long goodbye is necessary. Instead of letting it hold you back, put it On Hold and move on. You'll feel lighter right away, and every day your attachment will wane until you can let it go.

In
SPACE
cometh
GRACE.

JOHN HEYWOOD

organize

After you've dealt with your discards, it's time to organize what's left. You've done a lot of work consolidating items, and you want to prevent them from dispersing through the house again.

Organizing is simply giving each possession a proper place, so you know what belongs in your house and what doesn't. That's why it's very important this step come *after* you've curated. The last thing you want to do is organize your clutter!

For organizing, I like containers. They keep things consolidated and make it easy to put them away. That said, a container doesn't have to be a fancy box from an organization store. It can just as well be a drawer, closet, bookshelf, bag, or repurposed vessel — anything with fixed volume that keeps similar items together.

When things aren't contained, they drift around and pile up (in drawers, on tables, on counters) because there's nowhere to put them. That gives clutter the perfect place to hide. Conversely, when your chosen possessions have their own special spots, stray items stand out, making them easier to identify and remove. Things without a place don't belong in your space.

Containers give things a place to land when they enter the house — for instance, the basket in your foyer that catches winter hats and gloves, the hanging file in your kitchen that catches incoming paperwork, the tray on your dresser that catches loose change and keys.

Containers also make your stuff portable, giving you access to it wherever needed. If all your craft or office supplies are in a single box, you can set up a workspace anywhere in your house. When you're finished, simply scoop your stuff back into its container rather than leave it strewn on the table.

On a larger scale, well-contained stuff makes relocation easier. Instead of complete chaos on moving day, you can pack your stuff with less effort and angst. It also makes for a smoother transition when settling into your new home. Set up a good system, and you'll be able to move through the world with ease.

But here's the most wonderful thing about containers: They limit what you can keep. Restricting items to a certain space keeps your collection in check. If your container for socks or spices or small tools is full, you'll need to get rid of something before you add more (don't transfer them to a bigger one!).

When organizing, *let go of everything possible before containing it.* Then choose the smallest possible container to hold your stuff. Don't leave room for more if you want to have less. Consider containers a stopgap measure—a way to keep your stuff under control until you're ready to part with it. As you lighten up further, shrink the container size. The goal is to use smaller and smaller containers until you can eliminate them altogether.

Containers help you understand how much your life weighs. Just how heavy is that box of books or heirlooms or kitchen gadgets? What if you had to physically carry it with you everywhere you went? Are your possessions worth the weight they add to your life?

Organizing not only lightens your stuff, it lightens your stress. Once you've organized, you always know where everything is. Imagine that! No more frustration because you can't find your measuring tape, your favorite scarf, the receipt for something you need to return. No more running late or losing time because you're searching for "lost" things.

When you organize, you take control of your stuff, which in turn helps you take control of your life. You'll move through your daily routine more calmly and serenely. Getting ready for work, getting kids off to school, and getting dinner on the table is so much easier when everything's exactly where you need it.

Organizing isn't meant to hide things away, it's meant to put them in order once and for all. It makes all your wonderful, useful items easier to use. Just remember: The less you have to organize, the better. Life shouldn't be spent shuffling around stuff.

refine

The less you own, the more lightly you'll live. With that in mind, look for opportunities to further refine your stuff.

Don't worry, you don't have to fit everything into a backpack—or even close. *Any* refining you do will cast off some weight. And you know what usually happens next? You feel so exquisitely light and carefree, you're inspired to refine some more. Set a goal to stay motivated, like discarding one item each day or a total of one hundred (or one thousand) things. For support, announce your goal to family, friends, or your social network, and post updates on your progress.

But refining is more than decluttering; it's seeking out all kinds of ways to live with less. To that end, favor versatility in everything you own: multipurpose furniture, seasonless clothes that can be layered, shoes and handbags that go with everything, and pans that can cook a wide range of meals. Unlike single-task specialty gear, these workhorses rise to many occasions, so you won't have to own nearly as many things.

In fact, sometimes an item is so versatile, it's the only one you need. Imagine how lovely it would be to have one pair of sneakers or rain boots, one formal dress for special occasions, one bag that fits all your needs. One pen, one pot, one saucepan, one suitcase, one lipstick of the perfect shade. Go on and give it a try: It sounds extreme, but it's surprisingly doable (and also a lot of fun).

Refining is making smart choices based on your needs, rather than what everyone else has or what advertisers tell you to have. You likely own gear for things you think you *should* do —make your own pasta, sew your kids' clothes, power-wash your deck—but never get around to actually doing. Release those items and free up time and space for activities you actually enjoy.

Further refine your possessions by participating in the sharing economy: borrow books, rent an evening gown, use a tool library, join a car share program. If you need an item irregularly or infrequently, better to borrow than to own it.

Finally, take full advantage of modern technology and digitize what you can. For example, refine sentimental items by preserving the memories with pictures instead of the actual objects. Digital technology makes your paperwork, photographs, books, movies, music, games—and sometimes even heirlooms—absolutely weightless. You can enjoy them to your heart's content, whenever and wherever you want, without having to worry about physically storing or transporting them. It doesn't get any lighter than that.

Refining isn't something you do all at once. It's continually assessing your needs and fine-tuning your possessions: borrowing something here, digitizing something there, replacing a worn-out item with something more versatile. It's losing the weight bit by bit, ounce by ounce, by making Lightly a lifestyle.

reign

Your home is your personal kingdom. Reign over it wisely so that you—not your stuff—is in control.

A household is a complicated system; by nature, it tends to chaos if left unattended. A guiding hand is needed to keep things peaceable.

As king or queen of your castle, your first duty is to maintain order. Now that each possession has its own spot, always be sure it returns there. Stay vigilant over your tables, your countertops, your floor—all those lovely surfaces where clutter accumulates. Whenever you notice a stray item, show it to its proper place. Make sure everyone else in your household knows where to put stuff, too. It can help to label exactly where the salad plates, stapler, or school forms belong.

When things get unruly, do a reset: Restore your space to its pristine, uncluttered state. In other words, gather all the out-of-place items and put them away. Do this nightly or weekly—whatever helps you stay ahead of the mess. Involve your whole family, and make each person responsible for their own belongings.

Your second responsibility is to monitor entry. Your home is vulnerable to invasion—by gifts, junk mail, freebies, bargains, among other things—and must be protected. Be on guard during high-influx periods like holidays and end-of-season sales; that's usually when our defenses are down and our doors are open.

Be mindful of every last item that enters your home. The more you restrict the inflow, the easier this will be. First and foremost, buy less (more on that in Lighten Your Step). To deal with unsolicited items, you'll have to get more creative: unsubscribe from mailing lists, propose gift-free holidays, refuse giveaways, and pass politely on the hand-me-downs.

Before you stash anything away, stop and ask if you really want it in your household. Will it make your life heavier or lighter? If you welcome something new, maintain equilibrium with a like-for-like trade: a book for a book, a shoe for a shoe, a couch for a couch. Try your best not to *add* any weight to your home.

Finally, make Lightly the law of your land: Dethrone consumerism, and center your home and family life on values like community, creativity, generosity, and sustainability. Instead of spending your leisure time shopping, volunteer or write a novel. Teach your kids the joys of giving rather than getting. Take care not to make much waste or harm the environment.

Further these efforts by forming alliances. If you can interest your partner, children, parents, or peers in minimalism, all the better. Perhaps your mom will find less material ways to spoil the grandkids, and your best friend will consider alternatives to a gift exchange. Rather than preach, simply share the happiness *you've* found in living more lightly.

Set up a new hierarchy in your home — space over stuff, people over possessions — and tranquility will reign.

restraint

Marketers, advertisers, and society in general constantly urge us to consume—and the more, the better. In recent years, social media has added to the pressure: Trends move at lightning speed, and celebrities and influencers fill our feeds with the latest "must-haves." Where does that leave us? Weighed down with more clutter, more debt, and more stress in our efforts to keep up.

To live more lightly, practice restraint—it's a rare and beautiful thing in this age of excess. Restraint is elegant simplicity, living gracefully with just the essentials.

You don't have to stop shopping entirely; it would be impractical to grow or make all the food, clothes, furniture, and other goods you need. The problem is that we consume a lot of things we *don't* need. And not only does that clutter our homes, it wastes precious resources that all inhabitants of this planet (present and future) depend upon.

When you practice restraint, you limit your purchases to necessities. You buy less—much, much less. You buy a new sweater because your old one is worn out, a laptop because your work requires it, a chair because you need something to sit on—not because they're the newest trend, latest technology, or hippest design. You buy for function rather than novelty, need rather than want.

When you practice restraint, you make do with what you

have. You don't buy a new item if you have something else that can do the job; you see what you can repurpose or refashion to meet your needs.

When you practice restraint, you avoid buying specialty or single-task items. Instead, you favor versatile items that can perform a multitude of tasks (like a paring knife instead of a strawberry huller).

When you practice restraint, you borrow what you can and share your stuff with others. You recognize that you don't need to own everything, and would rather not purchase and possess items you rarely use.

When you practice restraint, you buy for the long term. You forgo cheap and trendy items in favor of those that are durable in construction and timeless in style. You want your stuff to last as long as possible, so you can use less of the earth's resources and put less into its landfills.

It's easy to practice restraint if you follow two basic principles. First, shop only when you need something. Spend your leisure time at the park instead of the mall, and don't browse catalogs or online stores looking for something to buy.

Second, avoid advertising in every way possible. It's designed to make us feel insecure and unsatisfied with what we have. Some ideas: stop the catalogs, turn off the television, use an ad-blocker in your browser. Shield your children from ads as well; they may be small, but they have a powerful influence over what you buy.

If restraint doesn't come easy to you, try this: Set a two-week waiting period before you purchase non-necessities. Sure, that cute dress or throw pillow may no longer be on sale, but you might also realize you really don't need it. Most likely, at the end of that time, you'll have forgotten all about it. And if you have buyer's remorse over a recent splurge, see if you can take it back—many retailers have generous return policies. Next time do your best not to act so impulsively.

Fortunately, when you make "Lightly" your mantra, shopping loses much of its appeal. You don't want more baggage to carry through life or declutter in the future. Before you hand over your credit card or click the "Buy" button, consider how the purchase might weigh you down. Will it put you in debt, take up too much space, or be hard to get rid of? Many an item is not worth the burden.

aparigraha

The Yoga Sutras of Patanjali outline five *yamas*—a list of self-restraints to help us live more ethical, enlightened, and harmonious lives. The first four are *ahimsa* (non-violence), *satya* (truthfulness), *asteya* (non-stealing), and *brahmacharya* (moderation). The fifth is *aparigraha,* which is the virtue of non-possessiveness or non-attachment.

Aparigraha is detailed in sutra 2.39, which says that once we conquer possessiveness, we can understand the "how and why of life." In other words, when we stop chasing our desires and grasping for more—be that a new dress, the latest smartphone, even an accolade or promotion—we can devote our time and energy to discovering what's really meaningful in life.

Aparigraha doesn't mean we can't own things, but rather that we're not attached to them. We're grateful for the necessities—our home, our car, our clothes, our laptop—but could gracefully let them go if a flood, fire, theft, or other circumstance took them away from us.

Instead of obsessing over what to buy next, we own just what we need and nothing extra. We don't covet, hoard, or cause harm with our consumption. We don't care about other people's stuff or show off our own. We focus less on having and more on being.

Aparigraha applies not just to our possessions, but to our relationships, ideas, and goals as well. Instead of being attached to specific situations or outcomes — or miserable when things don't turn out as we wished — we go with the flow and embrace events as they happen.

Aparigraha is a wonderful example of the multifaceted benefits of yoga — a practice that brings lightness not only of body, but of mind and spirit as well.

item by item
work clothes

For many of us, the largest part of our wardrobe is what we wear to work. We spend much of our week earning a living, and we need clothes that make us look neat and professional while on the job. Even if you work from home, you likely need a few items on hand for in-person meetings or presentations.

Our work clothes are the workhorses of our closet, but that doesn't mean we need an army of them. Ironically enough, the fewer clothes we have, the more put-together we're likely to look.

Remember, work isn't a fashion show. Our coworkers and clients are more interested in *how* we do our job, not in what we wear while doing it. And unless you wear the same thing every day (and more power to you if you do), it's highly unlikely anyone will notice a repeated outfit.

To lighten your work clothes, first separate them from what you wear on the weekend or to formal affairs. The goal: to build a mini capsule wardrobe specifically for the office.

First, decide how many work outfits you need; six to ten is a comfortable range. On the low side, six outfits give you a week's worth of clothes plus one extra. Rotated consecutively, that keeps you from wearing the same thing on the same day each week. It also provides a backup in case something gets sidelined with a rip or stain. On the high side, ten outfits give you two weeks of unique ensembles, probably the most that anyone needs.

Next, put together outfits from your pile of clothes: For six days, choose six bottoms and six tops that can mix and match. Divide your bottoms into pants and skirts, depending on your personal preference and style. If your goal is to have the tiniest wardrobe possible, opt for dresses. They cover both top and bottom, providing an effortless, stylish way to dress.

While choosing your pieces, first consider whether they fit you, flatter you, and suit your workplace.

When it comes to work clothes, fit is paramount. While you may be able to get away with something a bit too slouchy (or even a bit too tight) on the weekend, an ill-fitting garment looks unprofessional. Select only items that fit you well or that you will commit to having tailored.

Next, make sure every candidate for your work capsule flatters you. While you don't have to be a fashionista to make a good impression, it certainly helps to look your best. Feeling good in your clothes helps you radiate confidence while on the job.

Finally, keep only those clothes that are suitable for your workplace. In other words, eliminate anything that's too casual, too dressy, or otherwise inappropriate. If your office doesn't have a dress code, look to those in higher positions for clues on what to wear.

From this core of wearable items, use the following three criteria to curate the perfect work capsule.

First, choose classic styles over trendy ones. They look more polished and professional and have longer staying power in your wardrobe.

Second, opt for seasonless fabrics that are comfortable to wear in a wide range of temperatures. Most of us work in climate-controlled environments, and don't need separate summer and winter wardrobes for the workplace.

Third, select only comfortable clothes for your capsule. Workdays can be long and demanding, and the better you feel, the better you'll perform. You certainly don't want to be itching, tugging, pulling, or shifting when you're making a presentation or closing a deal.

For truly effortless dressing, take a cue from some of the world's most successful people and adopt a personal uniform (a signature style or ensemble you wear every day). This strategy eliminates decision fatigue—the exhaustion that results when you have to sort through a myriad of choices each morning. A uniform helps you start your day with ease and efficiency, saving your time and energy for more important matters.

If you have any clothes left over after creating your capsule, put as much as you can into your Out Box. Professional clothes are in high demand at charity shops and organizations like Dress for Success. When someone's struggling to get back on their feet, being able to secure a nice outfit for a job interview can help tremendously.

If you have items you're on the fence about, put them On Hold rather than back in your closet. See what it's like to live with only your capsule items. If you haven't retrieved anything after a few months, you'll feel much more comfortable letting them go.

In summary, eliminate anything that doesn't fit you, flatter you, or suit your workplace. Then favor pieces that are timeless, seasonless, and comfortable. Yes, it really is that simple to dress Lightly for work.

casual clothes

Casual clothes are what you wear on the weekend, while walking your dog, running errands, or lounging around the house — just about everything you do when not at work.

Be just as selective with your casual clothes as you are with your work clothes. However, because leisure time involves more outdoor activities, you'll likely need some season-specific pieces. My recommendation: Aim for four to six outfits for cold weather, and four to six outfits for warm weather. That allows for long sleeves and pants when it's chilly and lightweight garments when temperatures rise.

The key criteria in selecting your casual pieces: that they be comfortable, low-maintenance, and versatile.

First, choose clothes you can actually relax in. Nobody wants to kick back in business attire or make dinner in a pencil skirt. You want clothes that allow for plenty of movement so you can manage your grocery bags, maneuver your vacuum cleaner, and play with your kids. Easy silhouettes and forgiving fabrics (like those with a bit of stretch) maximize your comfort.

Next, make sure your casual clothes are low-maintenance. Don't include anything too fussy, precious, or difficult to launder. These pieces have to hold up to cooking, cleaning, children, pets, and the great outdoors. Select items that can be washed rather than dry-cleaned, and don't let worries about stains ruin your weekend fun.

Finally, keep versatility in mind. Opt for items you can wear outside the house as well as inside. Instead of a baggy sweatsuit, favor yoga pants and a fitted tee. Even if you're just going to the post office or grocery store, it's nice to look presentable.

The same goes for lounging around (or cleaning) your house. You don't have to vacuum in a dress and heels, but you should be able to answer your doorbell without embarrassment. Dressing comfortably yet neatly helps you maintain a sense of poise and elegance as you tackle your daily tasks.

Choosing your casual wear is easy—they're those favorite pieces you like to slip into after work or on your days off. If it helps, record what you wear for a week and see what patterns emerge.

Your bottoms will likely consist of chinos, jeans, yoga pants, or leggings. These are durable yet comfortable items that can hold up to a wide range of activities. Your tops will range from tees to more tailored styles that can go to brunch or a PTA meeting. You may opt to throw a casual dress or skirt into the mix. Paired with flip-flops, they can go to the beach; paired with heels, out on the town.

When you lighten up your leisure clothes, you won't get caught in something sloppy or shabby, and you won't waste your free time wondering what to wear.

formal clothes

How much formal wear should you have in your closet? No more than the number of events you typically attend each year. That means most of us can get by with one to three outfits. (If your life is more glamorous, add a few more.)

Here's how we end up with excess formal wear: When we have a black tie invitation in hand, we run out and purchase something special for the event. Afterward, we can't bring ourselves to get rid of it, no matter how unlikely it is that we'll wear it again. We paid good money for it, and it's just "so nice." Before long, we have a closet full of fancy clothes and no place to wear them.

Formal clothes are the least active items in our wardrobe. They're pressed into service every so often, but for most of the year, they simply hang around our closet looking pretty. Why keep them around at all? Because it's much less stressful to have an outfit on hand when that wedding invite arrives in the mail.

But even if you attend multiple affairs, one dress or suit may be all you need. Formal events are generally few and far between and have different people in attendance. You probably won't run into the same crowd at the opera, your cousin's wedding, and the gala fund-raiser for your child's school. And you know what's great about that? You can wear the same thing to all of them.

Therefore, choose your formal attire with year-round versatility in mind. Fortunately for us minimalists, dress clothes are generally seasonless. Men can wear the same suit or tuxedo all year, and women can get away with a strappy evening dress even in the middle of winter. Avoid summery prints and season-specific fabrics like velvet, and you'll be able to wear your party clothes any time of year.

When it comes to versatility, the little black dress is a time-honored classic. It's the easiest way to look stylish and chic at almost any event you attend. It also hides stains, so your night won't be ruined if someone spills a cocktail on you. If you have just one formal dress, the LBD is an excellent candidate.

But if black isn't for you, put a twist on the concept. Keep the style classic, but opt for a different color: A little red dress turns heads; a little blue dress is serene; a little gray dress has a quiet sophistication all its own. A lighter hue also covers those few occasions when the LBD might be out of place, like a brunch wedding or garden soirée.

And here's another idea: Consider a convertible dress. You can twist, wrap, and drape it into dozens of different looks: strapless, halter, one shoulder, short sleeve, cap sleeve, sleeveless, and much more. That way, you can wear the same dress to multiple events and always look different.

My crown is
IN MY HEART,
not on my head.

WILLIAM SHAKESPEARE

specialty clothes

Rounding out our wardrobes are specialty clothes — items that are specific to a hobby, task, or seasonal activity. They may be worn infrequently (like the bathing suit you take on vacation) or almost daily (like your running clothes).

Separate them from your regular wardrobe so you can consolidate and curate them appropriately. Consider their frequency of use to determine how many you need to keep. For example: If you're in the water only once or twice a year, you don't need a half dozen swimsuits. Pick your favorite one (or two) to keep, and make sure it fits you, flatters you, and makes you feel fabulous. Otherwise, you'll never want to wear it!

On the other hand, if you go jogging (or do yoga or play tennis) every day, keep enough outfits for one laundry cycle, be that a few days or a week. The same goes for gardening clothes, dance clothes, and any other task-specific apparel you have.

Curating your specialty clothes is a wonderful opportunity to evaluate your life. In other words, does your wardrobe match your reality?

Sometimes we keep apparel because we'd like to (or feel we *should*) engage in a particular activity, but we never do. Having a closet full of exercise clothes doesn't make you fit. If you're going to keep them, commit to going to the gym. The same goes for those ski pants languishing in the back of your closet; if you haven't hit the slopes in a decade, it's time to let them go.

You may also have some sentimental clothes — items you wore in the past but that no longer have any relevance to your life. It's hard to imagine a situation in which you might don that bridesmaid or prom dress again. Do you ever wear that college sweatshirt or those concert, tourist, or novelty tees? If not, take a photo of them for the memories, and send them on their way. Your wardrobe should be a celebration of your present, not an ode to your past.

When you dress Lightly, you keep only those things you actually wear — not the things you used to wear, would like to wear, should wear, or might wear if someday the stars align.

Remember, this isn't about giving up things you love to do. Keep those hiking pants if you're regularly on the trails, that leotard if you take a dance class, or that cosplay outfit if that's what you're into. It's important to have the right gear for your favorite activities. What you don't need is a bunch of extraneous clothes getting in the way and reminding you of what you're *not* doing — that just takes the fun out of everything. When you curate your specialty clothes, you identify what you truly enjoy and keep what you need to pursue it.

socks and underwear

Keep enough socks and underwear on hand so that you don't have to do laundry more often than necessary. For most people, a seven- to ten-day supply will suffice.

Men, you're all done here. Ladies, let's chat.

Why do we end up with so many undergarments? Because we have our comfortable stuff (which generally isn't sexy) and our sexy stuff (which generally isn't comfortable). The trick here is to strike a balance between the two, so that our undies are well suited to both routine and romantic occasions.

To this end, choose undies that are flirty and feminine but feel good to wear. A smooth and simple silhouette, trimmed with lace or other details, works well under clothes and still looks pretty. Keep ornamentation to a minimum or choose seamless pieces to avoid visible lines and unsightly bumps.

Four bras are a minimalist yet reasonable quantity that can cover your everyday needs; you may want a little more (or less) depending on your lifestyle, figure, and activities in which you engage. A convertible bra with detachable straps—so that it can be worn strapless, one strap, halter, cross-back, or classic style—eliminates the need for a handful of specialty bras.

Concerning shapewear: As a general rule, embrace your natural figure. Don't feel compelled to enhance, lift, or boost anything. You're beautiful just the way you are. That said, there are times when a little slimming and smoothing can make you feel more fabulous. Let's save that for slinky dresses and special occasions so we're not squeezing and squishing our bodies on a regular basis. Keep just a few versatile pieces that work under your clingiest clothes.

To lighten up your hosiery, stick to simple styles and hues. Ideally, each pair of socks, tights, and pantyhose should work with the majority of your wardrobe. Instead of having hosiery in a rainbow of colors, opt for neutrals like nude, gray, and black. Choose seasonless weights and textures that are appropriate year-round. I like cozy cable knits as much as the next girl, but they're much too warm much of the year.

It can be fun to indulge in novelty socks and tights, but they often spend most of their time in our closet. If you do, make it one pair at a time, and commit to wearing them out before getting another. That way, you can see if you actually enjoy wearing them as much as buying them. Otherwise, forgo cutesy motifs, fussy patterns, and anything that goes with only one outfit.

If you really want to go minimalist, consider whether you need hosiery at all. Depending on your climate and your workplace, you may be able to get away with a bare foot or leg on all but the coldest days.

outerwear

Choose your outerwear wisely, and you won't need a packed coat closet. With a few key pieces, you can be comfortable in any kind of weather.

Most important: Let climate, not fashion, determine your outerwear needs. That sounds obvious, but sometimes when we see that cute ski jacket in a catalog, we're tempted to purchase it—even if our weather rarely calls for such gear. Don't buy coats that stay home more than they get to go out.

When curating your outerwear, keep the following in mind: how your weather varies with the seasons, how low your temperature goes, and how wet your area gets. If you live in a four-season climate with frigid winters, you'll likely need a little more than those in milder regions.

If you're in a frosty part of the world, you'll need winter-specific outerwear. It's not fun or sensible to brave a Midwestern winter in a skimpy coat. No matter how minimalist you are, or aim to be, own a coat that keeps you warm on those freezing days. That said, having multiple winter coats doesn't keep you any warmer. You can wear only one at a time, so that's all you really need.

Of course, you may not want to wear your down parka to the opera or a five-star restaurant. If your lifestyle warrants it, keep a second winter coat—like a tailored wool one—for dressier occasions. That way, you'll have one for messy weather and snow shoveling, and one for dry days and date nights.

What to wear in fall and spring? The temperatures in these seasons are generally similar. Depending on where you live, one may be wetter than the other. But the idea that we need separate fall and spring coats is more a fashion thing than a weather thing.

One versatile coat can cover both of these seasons. A trench, for instance, can handle both spring showers and crisp autumn days. Stick to a neutral color — like gray, navy, or khaki — and it'll look chic any time of year. With a removable liner, it can even work for winters in milder climates.

And if you live someplace warm where the sun always shines, lucky you! A cardigan or wrap for cooler evenings may be the only bit of outerwear you need.

In summary: If owning one coat is your goal, make it a water-resistant shell with a removable liner that's warm enough for your winters. Otherwise, have one coat for winter and one for fall and spring. Consider anything else an "extra," and add according to your lifestyle.

For the rest of your outdoor accoutrements, try paring down to one: Keep just your favorite hat, your coziest scarf, a single pair of mittens or gloves. It saves space in your closet and saves time getting dressed for the elements. Do the same with umbrellas, sunglasses, sun hats, and other weather-related gear.

shoes

There's no magic number of shoes you should own—everyone's needs, lifestyles, and preferences are different. But know that if you want to live lightly, you can probably get by with a half dozen pairs.

Sound impossible? Take note of what you wear each day. You may have thirty pairs in your wardrobe but only five or six in regular rotation. We tend to wear our favorites (or most comfortable) all the time, and the others on rare occasions.

To determine which shoes are essential for you, consider the activities for which you need them. For the moment, forget about fashion and take a utilitarian approach.

You likely need shoes for the office. In most workplaces, a nice pair of flats or comfortable heels will do. Consider adopting a shoe uniform—a versatile style in a neutral color that goes with all your work clothes. You'll get out the door each morning in a flash; and unless you work at a fashion magazine, it's doubtful anyone will notice your footwear.

You'll also need some casual shoes to go grocery shopping, hang out with friends, or take your kids to the playground. Again, a pair or two will suffice; sneakers, sandals, flats, and loafers are all good options. For the most mileage, choose a classic style that can go from your backyard to brunch. Comfort is key; you don't want to rub a blister or hobble around in heels while enjoying a weekend stroll through the park.

It's nice to have a pair of dress shoes on hand, even if you need them just a few times a year. One pair can work if it's super-versatile, meaning it's appropriate for a professional function (like a job interview) as well as the fanciest event you might attend. It should also be seasonless so you can wear it year-round. For example, a slingback heel with a closed toe can go to the office or a party, in winter or summer.

If you'd really like to tread lightly, consider ballet flats. They're nice enough for the office, comfortable enough for the weekend, and can even be worn with formal wear. Simple and elegant, they'll pair with just about everything in your wardrobe. Imagine meeting almost all your footwear needs with a single pair of shoes!

Depending on your climate, you might need some bad-weather boots. Not only do they keep your feet cozy and dry, they spare your other shoes from the elements. When it comes to rain boots and snow boots, choose something that not only performs well but that you truly enjoy wearing. They'll bring a smile to your face on wet and wintry days.

If you'd like, choose an indulgence shoe — a dress boot, a flirty heel, a cute flat, a strappy sandal. Its primary function: to brighten your mood or boost your self-image. Just make sure it goes with more than one outfit and is a pair you actually wear.

handbags

For many of us, it's easy to go overboard on handbags. They're fun, they're trendy, and they're one-size-fits-all, making them an easy purchase when we want a quick pick-me-up.

But over time, those little bags add up to a big pile, and being bulky, they command quite a bit of storage space. We stash them on shelves, in closets, in nooks and crannies here and there. Not only does this create a clutter problem, it complicates our mornings with the extra decision of what to carry and the need to shift all our necessities (wallet, keys, lip gloss, phone, etc.) from bag to bag. And often, even with all those handbags at our disposal, we end up carrying the same one anyway.

It's very liberating to lighten up your bags. When you pare down to your favorites, you literally ditch a lot of extra baggage.

Start by selecting your everyday bag—the one that truly *works* for you on a daily basis. It's probably the one sitting by your door that you carried around today (and yesterday, and the day before that). It's the bag that fits everything you need when you're out and about—and if you're a parent, fits everything your little one needs, too.

Good candidates for an everyday bag are a shoulder bag, cross-body bag, or zippered tote. Ideally, it should keep your hands free to carry groceries, browse the bookstore, send a text, grab the pole on the subway, or hold on to your child. You don't want to have to set down your bag for a task that requires two hands.

The more versatile and durable your everyday bag, the better. It should be made of a stain-resistant and water-resistant material that can hold up to any weather or occasion. That way, you won't have to worry about your bag when you're in a crowded food hall or caught in a downpour. Choose a neutral color that works in every season and goes with everything in your wardrobe.

After choosing your everyday bag, consider what additional bags your circumstances call for. A work bag and evening bag are common essentials.

You'll need a work bag if you regularly transport your laptop, file folders, or documents back and forth from the office. These items require a more structured tote or brief that can accommodate their size and weight. Make sure it's strong, professional in style, and has enough pockets or compartments to keep your stuff organized. A detachable shoulder strap is a nice feature.

You may also need an evening bag for more formal affairs. Smaller, sleeker, and fancier than your everyday bag, your evening bag holds the bare essentials for a night out. A simple clutch is a classic choice; choose one with a wrist strap so you won't need to leave your bag unattended while dancing or mingling at a cocktail party. Opt for a neutral or metallic hue that complements all your formal wear.

Any handbags beyond that are usually just for variety. Consider whether they're worth the closet space they're occupying or if you'd be happier with a smaller supply. As you curate your collection, know that it's possible to live lightly with just one to three bags.

If that's not enough—or if you have a weakness for trendy or luxury bags—consider renting instead of buying. Numerous websites (like bagborroworsteal.com and renttherunway.com) will lend you that Chanel clutch, Hermès satchel, or latest It Bag so you can get your fix without the stress or expense of ownership. Rent for an event or by the month, and easily renew if you want to keep it longer. Some sites even offer subscription plans that allow you to borrow a certain number of items at a time and regularly refresh your collection. That way, you can indulge in all the variety you want without weighing yourself down.

Finally, keep your bag itself light: Do a weekly dump, and clear out all the spare change, loose wrappers, and receipts you've accumulated. It's not very elegant to drag around a heavy bag or dig through its depths when you need something. Curate its contents, and make sure you can reach in and pull out anything with ease.

accessories

Accessories can add a lot of mileage to your capsule wardrobe. Add a colorful scarf, bold necklace, or interesting belt to that black sheath, and it looks like a whole new outfit. Better yet, they're small and easy to store. A handful of accessories can multiply your looks exponentially while taking up no more closet space than a single sweater.

Because of their compact size, though, they often grow out of control. And it's no fun to waste your morning searching for that matching scarf, or combing through a pile of earrings to find your favorite pair.

To lighten up your accessories, consolidate and curate. Gather all candidates of a particular type — like scarves, belts, hats, or jewelry — and line them up across your bed. Consider each one in turn: Determine how much you like it, how often you wear it, and how many outfits it goes with. Whittle them down to a handful of favorites.

How much you keep depends on how minimalist you want to be. A general guideline (for each category) would be one to five pieces on the low side, six to ten on the high side. Alternatively, try cutting your collection in half. If you have twenty scarves, select your best ten; if you have a dozen bracelets, choose your favorite six. It can be helpful to recite "one to keep, one to give away" as you sort through your pieces.

Another option: Set a space limit on your accessories. Keep the number of scarves or belts that fit in the box or on the hanger you've devoted to them, and the amount of jewelry that fits in a small zippered case (rather than a large jewelry box). Paring down your jewelry to a few special pieces has a number of benefits: it's easier to keep track of them, decide which to wear, and hide them away for security. In fact, simply having less to steal can lift a huge burden from your mind.

Fortunately, accessories are easier to rehome than many other possessions. They're small enough to sell online and ship in an envelope. They make wonderful gifts, as they suffer little wear and tear and are often in like-new condition. They're also a charity shop favorite: They have wide appeal, take up little space, and (especially in the case of jewelry) can bring in a nice amount of money for their cause.

Have fun with your baubles, but remember to accessorize lightly—you don't want to jingle and jangle or look like a Christmas tree. For an elegant look, wear just one to three accessories at a time; let particularly bold statement pieces (a large belt, a bib necklace) stand alone. Accessories should complement, not compete with, your outfit and each other.

design

Your surroundings can greatly influence your mood. Don't be weighed down by cluttered rooms and ponderous furnishings. Create lightness in your home, and you'll invite more of it into your life. How to start? Look to Scandinavian, Shaker, and Japanese interiors for inspiration.

The Nordic countries are known for their bright and airy interiors, which maximize natural light during long, dark winters. White walls and pale wood floors create a sense of spaciousness, and provide a serene backdrop for streamlined furniture and carefully curated décor. Natural materials, cozy textiles, and selective pops of color add warmth and whimsy. The overall effect is light, lovely, and very *lagom*—a Swedish concept meaning "just the right amount."

Shaker interiors are all about simplicity. The religious sect, formed in the eighteenth century, prized humility, practicality, and freedom from materialism, and their homes reflected their values. Colors are muted, wood is favored, and ornamentation is minimized. Peg rails—for hanging coats, hats, tools, baskets, chairs, and more—keep floors clear and clutter at bay. Interestingly enough, Shaker-style cabinets are one of the most popular choices in kitchens today. How's that for timeless design?

Japanese design can make even the smallest home feel spacious and uncluttered. Clever storage hides necessities, and low-slung furniture makes rooms look bigger. Sliding screens lighten the interior and create a flexible floor plan with multi-purpose rooms. Embrace the concept of *kanso*—meaning simplicity, or paring down to the essential—for a calm, uncluttered, Zen-like retreat.

Browse Pinterest, Houzz, and Instagram to see what aesthetic speaks to you; but instead of buying new things, use the ideas to work with what you already have. A little decluttering, plus a little design inspiration, can go a long way toward lightening your home.

plates and bowls

Many of us have cabinets packed with dishes we never use, whether they're old ones we've replaced with something better, heirloom sets we've inherited, or wedding china that's "too good to use." They sit in our cupboards and rarely see the light of day, but they take up a lot of space, crowding out the stuff in daily rotation. Furthermore, they're heavy and fragile, making them a particular hassle to pack up every time we move.

Don't let excess dinnerware weigh you down; you can set an elegant table with just the essentials.

Keep the amount of plates and bowls that is appropriate for your family size and the number of people you regularly entertain. You want to easily accommodate visitors, but you don't need enough for a banquet (unless you actually intend to host one). Most households can get by with six to eight place settings — enough for family members and a couple of guests.

To keep your dishware to a minimum, versatility is key. For plates, choose a shape and size that's suitable for a wide variety of meals, like one with a sloping rim or shallow depression that can hold saucy food. A standard dinner plate may be all you need; if necessary, supplement with a smaller size for salads or desserts.

For bowls, make sure they'll hold soup, oatmeal, cereal, and dessert in the proportions you prefer. Medium-sized is a good choice, as moderate servings are a graceful approach to meals; you (or your guests) can always have seconds if desired.

In terms of design, choose a style that works for both everyday and entertaining. Avoid seasonal or novelty motifs that are out of place a large part of the year; dress your holiday table with natural décor (pine cones, pumpkins, flowers) instead of themed dishware.

Classic white or glass dinnerware fits every occasion and puts the focus on the food. For maximum utility, opt for pieces that are safe to use in the microwave and dishwasher.

When you need new dinnerware, buy it by the piece. Sets often contain more than we need and serving pieces we seldom use. Yet we're reluctant to pare it down, lest we break a piece and need a replacement. Better to choose an open-stock style and purchase (and replace) single pieces as needed.

A charming alternative: Embrace the bohemian look of mismatched dishware. It makes for an eye-catching table, and you'll never have to worry about discontinued patterns. When you crave novelty, you can indulge in a single place setting in a different style (instead of a whole new set).

In fact, this strategy is a wonderful solution if you have multiple sets and can't decide which to keep. Save a few pieces of your grandma's china, a few pieces from your wedding set, and a few other favorites you've collected over the years. That way, you can enjoy them all without the excess.

drinkware

Have you ever counted the number of cups and glasses in your kitchen cabinets? Drinkware multiplies in mysterious ways. We don't go out and purchase dozens of glasses at once, but somehow they accumulate over the years. We buy some for daily use and some for special occasions; others we receive as gifts or freebies.

Before we know it, we have a special glass for every type of drink: water glasses, juice glasses, wine glasses, pint glasses, whiskey glasses, margarita glasses, and those champagne glasses we bring out once or twice a year. And because they usually come six in a set, we have far too many of all of them.

Coffee cups proliferate as well. Our collection might range from the utilitarian mug to the more refined after-dinner cup; some might sport slogans, sayings, and other witticisms.

You might start to wonder: How many vessels do you really need to drink from? If you want to live lightly, not that many. Like dishware, drinkware takes up a lot of cabinet space, and it's no fun to pack, transport, and unpack a million cups each time you relocate.

To lighten up, switch to simple glass tumblers that accommodate every beverage. Opt for a versatile size (like eight- to twelve-ounce) and a classic design that works for any occasion. And unless you're a connoisseur, don't worry about special glasses for wine. Throughout Europe, restaurants serve their vintages in simple tumblers rather than fancy stemware.

For warm beverages, choose a cup that can go from the breakfast table to a dinner party. In other words, you don't want to be sipping your morning joe from a demitasse cup; nor do you want to serve an after-dinner drink in your "#1 Mom" mug. A simple shape and timeless design will do it all.

As with plates, buy singles rather than sets. You can then indulge in a variety of designs without the excess. Guests often delight in having a unique pattern, and it helps them keep track of their drink while mingling. Furthermore, you won't have to worry about finding a match when you inevitably break one (or two, or three).

Of course, you don't have to buy new drinkware in your quest to pare down. Very likely, you already have plenty of candidates that fit these criteria. Select your favorite and most versatile from among your collection and declutter the rest. The next time you need replacements, keep these guidelines in mind.

Don't forget that those cups and glasses can be pressed into service for food as well. Use them for yogurt, granola, or a small portion of soup. They're also an elegant way to serve dessert (like fruit, ice cream, mousse, or parfait).

flatware

If your utensil drawer is packed to the hilt, lighten up your flatware. You'll gain some space and set the table more quickly and efficiently.

First decide which utensils suit your family's eating habits. Most of us don't need a different fork for every food (fish fork, meat fork, strawberry fork, oyster fork), specialty knives (luncheon knife, dessert knife, fruit knife), or spoons in a half dozen sizes.

For the typical household, a dinner knife, dinner fork, soup spoon, and teaspoon are sufficient. They're the most versatile sizes and can handle just about anything you eat. You might add a smaller salad or dessert fork, particularly if you serve multi-course meals.

Once you've determined your requirements, lay out all your utensils on the dining table and start sorting. Make piles for each type you've decided to keep, and put the oddballs in your Out Box.

Next, decide how many place settings you need; generally, you'll want the same amount as your dinnerware. If you entertain often, you might opt for a few extras, in case a teaspoon goes missing or someone drops a fork on the floor during a dinner party. Go through each category of flatware, and narrow down to that number.

If you eat (or entertain) family style, you'll need a few serving pieces as well—an oversized fork and spoon will usually suffice. Add a slotted spoon and ladle if needed.

As you go through your cutlery, note the material it's made out of. For the easiest care, choose stainless steel. While sterling silver looks lovely, it requires a great deal of upkeep and accessories (polish, cloths, special storage containers) to keep it in top condition. You might not want to devote such effort to your eating implements.

Consider style as well. Novelty motifs have limited use, while a classic pattern suits any occasion. Your design of choice should be appropriate for both casual and formal meals.

As with dishware, mix and match to your heart's content for a lovely, eclectic look (and no worries about discontinued patterns). If you have multiple sets, save a few place settings from each, or pick up interesting vintage or artisan pieces when you find them. When you host a gathering, your flatware itself may become a topic of conversation. Guests will love to hear that their spoon is from your nuptials, their knife is from a grand old hotel, or their fork has been in your family since the 1920s.

And by all means, use that heirloom, wedding, or other fancy set if you have one. Don't wait for a "special occasion." Each day we open our eyes is cause for celebration. Enjoy your best stuff every day of your life.

HAPPINESS

is not found in things

you possess, but

in what you

HAVE THE COURAGE

TO RELEASE.

NATHANIEL HAWTHORNE

entertaining ware

You're probably wondering what to do with those serving pieces — like the gravy boat, cake stand, or punch bowl — that rarely make an appearance. They sometimes emerge around the holidays, but spend most of the year gathering dust in your cabinets. Or perhaps you're reluctant to purge those extra place settings, imagining someday you might throw a big soirée.

When you want to lighten up, the prospect of holidays and entertaining can be daunting. You don't want to store rarely used items, yet you want them on hand if you need them.

You can address this problem in one of two ways. First: Be a borrower. Declutter those dormant pieces, and don't worry about it until you have to. This strategy works well if you seldom entertain. In the rare case you're asked to host a holiday dinner, call up your mother or sister or friend to borrow that soup tureen or tablecloth.

Don't feel the need to supply everything on your own; loved ones are usually more than happy to contribute to the festivities. Such sharing brings an extra sense of warmth, love, and community to your table. Just remember: If you borrow a serving platter from your neighbor, be sure to invite her to dinner. If you're really in a jam, throw a potluck. Not only is it great fun, everyone will bring their contribution in their own serving dish.

You can also turn to a party rentals company. They'll supply everything you need—chairs, tables, linens, dishware, glass-ware, flatware, décor, and more. You don't have to host a large affair, like a banquet or wedding, to use their services. Many places rent by the piece, with low or no minimums, making them a good resource for smaller gatherings, too.

The second option: If you entertain regularly, keep what you use on hand. Regularly doesn't have to mean every weekend; it can be once a year, when you host that annual Thanksgiving dinner or Easter brunch. If it'd be inconvenient to track down a roasting pan each November, make your peace with owning (and storing) one.

To keep things light, keep them out of the way. In other words, gather those seldom-used pieces into their own special place—like that hard-to-reach cabinet above the refrigerator. If you're short on cupboards, you can even keep them in a storage box in another part of the house. That way, they won't take up precious kitchen space or get in the way of your everyday cook-ing; yet they'll be waiting in the wings, ready for action when you need them.

pots and pans

Do you really need all the pots and pans knocking about your cabinets? Or might you be able to get by with a few well-chosen pieces of cookware?

Pots and pans claim a lot of cupboard space. They're large, heavy, and awkward to store (and even harder to pack when moving). But never fear: You can pare down your cookware and still make all your favorite meals.

The Lightly approach: Make a core collection of your favorite and most versatile pots and pans. Because cookware is often sold in sets (or we combine households with a partner), we end up with fry pans, saucepans, and other pieces in various sizes. Yet we usually reach for the same one time and again—that one magic size that's comfortable to maneuver and fits everything we like to cook. As you curate your cookware, keep the one size of each type you use most often; add a second size only if you use it on a regular basis.

The following are some popular choices for a minimalist, hard-working set of cookware. Of course, feel free to vary the pieces based on your own culinary preferences.

Most households will need a frying or sauté pan. If you'd prefer just one, consider a chef's pan—a deep, multipurpose pan with sloping (rather than straight) sides. It sears, sautés, stews, stir-fries, browns, braises, and reduces sauces. The sides keep in liquids (like a traditional sauté pan) yet allow for tossing on the stovetop. It can also be used in the oven. Look for full-clad construction, rather than a disk bottom, for even distribution of heat.

A saucepan is another kitchen workhorse—handy not only for making sauces but for heating soup, boiling eggs, steaming vegetables, making small batches of pasta, and cooking rice, oatmeal, and other grains. A three-quart size is ideal for a couple or small family; you can go slightly smaller or larger according to your needs. For even more versatility, consider a saucier. It has curved walls rather than straight sides, making for easier stirring, whisking, and cleaning.

Most lists of kitchen essentials also include a large (eight- to twelve-quart) stockpot for making big batches of pasta or stock. While some households may find this necessary, others don't need such a huge pot. For the latter, a five- or six-quart multipot is a good alternative. For a small family, it's roomy enough for boiling pasta, potatoes, spinach, and leafy greens, and much easier to manage.

Finally, you might want to keep an alternative pan for cooking eggs, quesadillas, pancakes, French toast, and other foods that tend to stick to stainless steel. A pan with a nonstick coating is inexpensive, lightweight, and easy to clean; however, the coating can flake over time and pose a health risk. Cast iron is a chef's favorite; it must be seasoned, but with proper care and cleaning, it can last forever. The only drawback: it's very heavy, so it can be difficult to maneuver and transport. Carbon steel is a happy medium. It's similar to cast iron but is slimmer and lighter, making it a good choice for mobile lifestyles.

If you're a serial mover or living in a small space—like a boat, studio, or tiny home—you may want to consider a nested set of cookware. Removable handles and interchangeable lids allow a stockpot, saucepan, and sauté pan to stack together like a Russian doll (be still, my nomadic heart). Such a compact package makes for easy transport or storage in a tiny kitchen.

Beyond these core pieces, let your menu be your guide. Keep that paella pan, pressure cooker, or Dutch oven if your cooking requires it. Lightly means paring down to your personal essentials. As long as they're in regular use, they're welcome in your kitchen.

bakeware

How much bakeware you need depends on your sweet tooth and the quantities you bake. If you're regularly making goodies for bake sales and birthday parties, you'll need more apparatus than someone with an occasional craving.

At the very least, you'll likely want the standard half-sheet pan: a thick, rimmed, one-inch-deep aluminum cookie sheet measuring eighteen by thirteen inches. It's not just for cookies; use it to roast vegetables, cook fish, bake bread, toast nuts, and make oven fries. It can also accommodate bars, brownies, granola, bacon, and entire sheet-pan suppers. Line it with parchment paper for a nonstick surface.

If you bake infrequently, a half-sheet pan may be all you need. But for those with sweeter ambitions, a bigger arsenal of bakeware may be in order. As always, base your choices on your personal preferences. If you regularly eat pies, muffins, or zucchini bread, keep what you need to make them.

The same goes for the stand mixer, Bundt pan, candy thermometer, cookie cutters, and frosting tips. Curate your own collection of must-have equipment. Just don't feel obligated to be *able* to make a layer cake if you likely never will.

If you'd prefer to lighten up your bakeware, explore other ways to satisfy your sweet tooth. For example, instead of baking a big cake or two dozen cookies, patronize your local bakery to get your fix. That way, the excess won't go stale (and you won't be tempted to overindulge). You'll also be able to soak in the ambience, engage with your community, and try treats you might never have made yourself.

Alternatively, get creative with small-batch baking. Miniature cookie, cake, and muffin pans make just the right amount for a single person or couple. Use a tart pan to make tiny pies, and ramekins for mini cakes, cobblers, and cornbread. This diminutive bakeware takes up little space and can even be used in a toaster oven. Plus, you can mix small batches of batter by hand, eliminating the need for heavy-duty equipment.

Just note: You can't simply halve or quarter a brownie recipe and expect good results. Seek out cookbooks and websites dedicated to small-batch baking. They'll have recipes that are properly scaled down and tested for tiny quantities. It's lovely to make just a small plate of cookies, with no worries about any going to waste.

And for the ultimate in no-fuss baking, make mug cakes. These single-serving delights can be mixed up with a fork in your favorite coffee mug, and baked in minutes in your microwave. Search the Internet for recipes, and have a blast whipping up wee versions of red velvet, caramel apple, or molten chocolate cake, and more. Preparation and cleanup are a snap, and you get to indulge in a sweet treat with built-in portion control.

small appliances

If you often wish for more counter or cabinet space, pare down your small appliances. They're bulky, tough to store, and take up some serious kitchen real estate. Such equipment can be convenient: You can whip up a cappuccino on a whim or bake bread with the push of a button. But oftentimes, the setup and cleanup of such machines dampen our enthusiasm to use them; so they sit idly on our counters or in the darkness of our cupboards, waiting for that rare occasion when we give them a whirl.

When curating your kitchen, give due consideration to how often you actually use these items. Some completely justify the space they claim: If you use your electric kettle every day, your rice cooker once a week, or your waffle iron once a month, it has reason to be in your kitchen. On the other hand, if you drag out that deep fryer or food processor just once or twice a year—or can't even remember using the electric griddle—you'll have a lighter kitchen without them.

Not only do fewer appliances make for a more spacious kitchen, they also make for a quieter one. In our modern era, we're accustomed to things beeping, buzzing, and whirring around us. It's almost second nature to plug into an electrical outlet and let a machine complete our tasks. But there's something to be said for mindful cooking. It's quite satisfying to chop, knead, mix, and mince with your own two hands. Working by hand, instead of machine, connects you to your food and nourishes your soul. It makes the process of cooking less mechanical and more meditative. And in many cases, the results taste better.

Therefore, consider low-tech alternatives to the machines in your kitchen. For example, use a mortar and pestle instead of a food processor; it crushes ingredients more gently, releasing their oils and retaining more flavor, aroma, and texture. Try a pour-over dripper instead of a coffee maker; it makes for a lovely morning ritual and a cleaner, richer, more flavorful brew. Knead your bread dough by hand instead of machine; it gives you more control over the finished loaf and a blissful sensory experience.

Remember, delicious doesn't have to be complicated. Instead of an elaborate sauce, garnish your dish with a squeeze of lemon or sprinkle of herbs. Instead of pulverizing them in a food processor, serve your fruits, nuts, and vegetables whole. People have been making tasty food for thousands of years without electric appliances.

Simplifying your kitchen has another wonderful side effect: It takes a lot of weight off your culinary shoulders. When you don't have the apparatus to cook anything and everything, you don't feel the pressure to do so. You don't feel obligated to tackle complicated recipes, nor do you have to operate and clean an assortment of machines. A lighter kitchen can make you feel more relaxed, and bring new joy and creativity to your cooking.

kitchen tools

How crowded are your kitchen drawers? When you're elbow deep in a recipe, you want to be able to grab what you need at the moment you need it.

When you lighten up your gadgets and tools, you won't have to rummage around for your favorite whisk or most-loved measuring spoons. Your chosen items will be nestled in their designated spots, awaiting their call to service instead of buried beneath a pile of less useful things.

First, consolidate each category of kitchen tool — spatulas, knives, peelers, graters — and cull the duplicates. You might be surprised at how many corkscrews or wooden spoons you have. When we acquire a new one, we rarely get rid of the old. Instead, we keep them as backups "just in case" our favored ones fail. The problem is, they crowd out our good stuff and get in the way when we're cooking. Let go of the multiples. I promise, you won't miss them. Honor your most-treasured kitchen tools by giving them some breathing room.

Have fun singling out the best and most versatile tool in each category. Instead of keeping multiple whisks, choose the one with loops numerous enough to beat eggs yet sturdy enough to mix batter. Choose the turner that's strong enough for sandwiches yet leaves the flakiest fish intact. Choose the grater that can handle citrus, carrots, and cheese with ease.

Remember, functionality trumps sentimentality. Keep the can opener that cuts like a dream rather than the subpar one you received as a wedding gift. Skip the novelty motifs — the heart-shaped measuring cups, the holiday-themed spatula — and opt for tools that are made to perform.

Furthermore, don't feel you have to keep everything in a set. Just because a dozen knives came in that fancy block doesn't mean you need all of them. Narrow down to the most versatile, such as a paring knife, serrated bread knife, and chef's knife in a comfortable size (eight-inch is a popular choice). In the future, buy your tools singly rather than in sets, so you can select the items most useful for you.

Further lighten up by eliminating the single-taskers in your kitchen, those tools that are so specialized, they can't be used for much else. An olive pitter, apple corer, or banana slicer may be good at what it does, but a knife can do the same job and leave you with more space in your drawers.

If you're still unsure of what to keep, try this: Empty your drawers of all of your kitchen tools. Keep them in a box outside the space but easily accessible. As you go about your daily cooking, retrieve what you need and return it to your kitchen. After a few weeks, you'll see what you use on a regular basis and what you can do without.

junk drawer

It's hard to imagine curating your junk drawer. Few of us treasure the chopsticks, toothpicks, old keys, and other odds and ends that usually get stashed there.

No worries—from now on, call it your utility drawer. Make it a new, lighter repository of the things you find truly useful to have on hand.

Separate the hard-working items from the detritus, and give them a proper place in a container or drawer organizer. That's all it takes to create a go-to collection of small tools and miscellany that are readily available when you need them.

The key to a lighter, more organized utility drawer is to give everything a place. It prevents loose items from rolling around and becoming a mess, and wayward objects from ending up there. Don't shove something into your utility drawer because there's nowhere else to put it; first, question whether you need to keep it at all. If so (and if there isn't a better spot for it), carve out a designated place—like a container, slot, or compartment—into which it can settle.

Stack your favorite takeout menus in a neat pile (or binder clip), and you have a working directory of local food options for busy evenings.

Consolidate batteries in a small container, so you won't have to search the house for a triple-A the next time a toy or gadget runs out of juice.

Gather all the birthday candles and matchbooks so they're easily accessible for your next celebration.

Keep a small bag to collect spare change instead of letting it accumulate around the house. Once it's full, cash it in at the bank and have dinner out (or start a fund for something special, like a vacation, holiday gifts, or a savings goal).

Put together a repair kit with the sewing needles, spare buttons, eyeglass screws, and other parts you need to fix things.

Consolidate fasteners like twist-ties, bag clips, rubber bands, and safety pins so you can put your hands on them with ease.

Keep an envelope for coupons if you use them, or receipts if you don't have a better place for them. Purge them periodically to eliminate anything outdated.

A utility drawer needs regular maintenance: Give it a good clean-out at least twice a year, like at the start of spring and fall. That way, you can stay on top of its contents and flush out anything that snuck its way in. Remove items that are old, expired, unused, or unidentifiable, and those that belong somewhere else in the house.

Once your utility drawer is no longer a catchall for everything, it can serve a truly useful purpose: making your life easier by supplying just what you need when you need it.

walden

Intrigued by the idea of living with just the essentials? Curl up in your favorite reading chair with *Walden*, by writer and philosopher Henry David Thoreau. Published in 1854, it chronicles his two-year experiment in Spartan simplicity — living in a one-room cabin he built by hand in the woods outside Concord, Massachusetts.

His furnishings consisted of a desk, a table, a bed, and three chairs: "one for solitude, two for friendship, three for society." Other than that, he possessed little more than a handful of cooking and eating implements, even doing away with three pieces of limestone on his desk because they required daily dusting.

Thoreau was a leading figure in Transcendentalism, a philosophical and literary movement that arose in early 1800s' New England. The Transcendentalists valued self-reliance, independence, and a deep reverence for nature. They were very spiritual but saw no need for organized religion, believing in the unity and divinity of all creation (humankind included).

Walden is a detailed and delightful account of Thoreau's attempt "to live deliberately, to front only the essential facts of life." He dresses simply, eats lightly, thinks deeply, and lives not by the clock but by the rhythms of nature. He steps back from the expectations and distractions of society and lives fully in the present, savoring every moment.

Walden is a classic text on living lightly, and is more relevant than ever in this age of consumerism and digital distraction. It reminds us to slow down, disconnect, and appreciate the wonder and beauty of the world around us. And while you may not be ready to live off the grid, it might inspire you to take a tech-free weekend or vacation, or to cast off some of your own "accumulated dross" and downsize to a smaller home.

office supplies

Thankfully, in our digital age, we need far fewer office supplies than in days of yore. Now that we conduct much of our business electronically, supply closets full of pens, paper clips, envelopes, notepads, staples, and other physical paraphernalia are no longer necessary. Shed those office supplies you'll probably never use. A more spacious and serene workspace can do wonders for your productivity.

Start with a Clean Slate: Empty the drawers or boxes where you store these items. It's too tedious to pick through them, looking for stuff to throw away. Dump them out, and put back only what you actually use.

As you curate your office tools, get rid of the multiples. Choose your favorite stapler, ruler, pencil sharpener, pair of scissors, etc. to keep. You don't need backups for things that are inexpensive and easy to replace.

Be honest about whether you really use each item. You may not have touched that hole punch or clipboard in ages and rarely have need for those index cards, push pins, and binder clips. The same goes for office supplies that are truly obsolete. Take this opportunity to say goodbye to the fax paper and floppy disks still languishing in your desk.

Even if you still use pens, paper clips, and other office consumables, you don't need enough for a lifetime. In all likelihood, you use far fewer than in the past. Keep just a small stash on hand for the occasions you need them. Instead of buying them in bulk, save the ones that come your way — the rubber bands around your mail, the paper clips on your kids' schoolwork — and put them back in circulation. Unless you're running a full-fledged business out of your home, you can probably fit everything you need in a small zippered case.

The best way, by far, to lighten your office supplies is to be as paperless as possible. The fewer papers you have, the fewer things you need to file them, staple them, clip them, mail them, and otherwise corral them. Therefore, at every turn and for every task, consider electronic alternatives to generating a paper trail. E-mail documents, pay bills online, download statements digitally, and print as little as possible. One day, you may even consider a stapler obsolete.

In fact, once you clear your desk of all those office supplies, you may find you no longer need a desk — or even a home office. You might prefer to work from your sofa or kitchen table, or if you'd like a little camaraderie, from a coworking space like WeWork. A shared workspace gives you access to the Internet and business equipment (like printers and paper shredders). It's a novel way to work lightly and pursue your professional dreams without the expense and trappings of a formal office.

paperwork

Starting today, resolve to live as paperlessly as possible. Instead of printing and requesting hard copies, conduct your transactions electronically and save your files digitally. That way, you'll have far less paperwork to deal with in the future.

So how can you clear out the papers stacked on your desk and stashed in your file cabinet? With the Lightly filing system. Using just five components, you can pare down your papers and organize them properly.

1. **Recycling bin.** Use it for the junk mail, circulars, advertisements, and other unimportant papers that enter your life. Put them in here before they land on your coffee table or kitchen counter. "Expired" papers whose information has become outdated or irrelevant—old receipts, newsletters, articles, flyers—belong here as well. (Shred any documents that contain personal information.)

2. **Scanner.** If you need the information but not the actual piece of paper, use a scanner or app to digitize it. Scanning is a wonderful way to "save" articles, letters, greeting cards, pamphlets, statements, and more without taking up an inch of space. To avoid digital clutter, be selective in what you scan, and back up your files regularly (to an external hard drive or the cloud) so you don't lose your data.

3. **Action file.** Designate a special place—like a wall-mounted vertical file in your foyer, kitchen, or office—for papers that need action. It's for bills that need to be paid (like utility and credit card statements), documents that need a signature or reply (like invitations and permission slips), and notices that need noting on your calendar (like school and community events). Make sure these papers leave your action file after you've dealt with them.

4. **Yearly file.** This file box or accordion folder is for documents you've dealt with but need to keep for the short term (generally a year or less). Candidates include recent receipts, bills, and financial statements. For example, keep a year's worth of utility bills on file, and toss last May's when you receive this May's. Keep receipts in here until the return period has passed or you no longer own the item. Think of your yearly file as a revolving door, with new papers coming in and old papers going out. Store it close at hand so you can add and remove documents with little fuss.

5. **Archive file.** Keep a separate file box or accordion folder for the papers you're stuck with long term. That might mean seven years, as for most tax-related items, or indefinitely, for insurance policies, real estate records, loan documentation, annual investment statements, and the like. Also include birth certificates, marriage certificates,

diplomas, deeds, and other documents that prove your identity, significant events, or major transactions. (If they'd be difficult to replace, consider storing them in a fireproof or safe-deposit box.)

That's it! Simply route your papers into one of these five channels, and prevent them from piling up around the house. If one of the files starts to overflow, don't start another; purge the old to make room for the new. Instead of accumulating more papers as you go through life, make it your goal to have less. Print to PDF files, sign up for electronic delivery, and cull your current stash.

The less paperwork you have, the easier it is to keep track of what's important. With this system in place, you'll always have a compact, well-edited collection of your most essential documents.

tech devices

We're lucky to live in a digital age. Today's technology can make our lives easier and eliminate a host of possessions from our households. The goal is to accomplish as many tasks as possible with a few well-chosen devices. Don't buy gadgets for novelty's sake or because everyone else has them. Own only those that truly add value to your life.

A laptop, for example, can function as an entire virtual office. Not only can it be used for your actual job — writing, designing, researching, illustrating, programming, number-crunching, or whatever it is you do — it's a powerful tool for marketing your business and communicating with clients.

By managing documents and administrative matters digitally, you can create an almost paperless workspace — eliminating the need for envelopes, paper clips, and countless other supplies. You may even be able to forgo a file cabinet, desk, or dedicated office. When you can work from your dining table or local coffee shop, you can live in a smaller space and perhaps even avoid a daily commute.

A laptop can also serve as your entertainment center. It can store or stream your music, movies, and favorite shows, so you can do away with the television and physical media (and the furniture they require). Use it to store books and photos digitally, and you can eliminate hundreds of pounds of possessions.

If you don't need a full-fledged computer at home, consider

a tablet. It performs many laptop functions (e-mail, web surfing, music, movies, and more) in a smaller package. Its compact form also makes it an ideal e-reader, and enables you to keep an entire library on a device thinner and lighter than a single book.

Finally, a smartphone is more than a communication device. It functions as a camera, calculator, calendar, notepad, GPS, music player, web browser, time-keeping tool, and so much more, making redundant items unnecessary. With the growing number of apps, it becomes more versatile each day and can even eliminate other office equipment. You can replace your scanner with a scanning app, and reduce your need for a home printer by using an electronic signature app and downloading coupons, tickets, boarding passes, and other documents to your phone.

To consume lightly, don't upgrade every time a new model comes out. Stick with your current device until it conks out or no longer runs the apps or software you need. When you replace it, don't keep the old one "just in case"—pass it along to someone else, donate it to a women's shelter or senior center, or responsibly recycle it.

Replace an office with a laptop, bookshelves with a tablet, and any number of gadgets with a smartphone. It's pretty amazing how a few devices can lighten up your stuff! Just make sure any device you own is a true workhorse and not just a distraction.

Simplicity
never fails to charm.

HONORÉ DE BALZAC

digital

Storing things digitally is a marvelous way to reduce our physical possessions. It's liberating to have documents, letters, books, photos, games, movies, and music that are literally as light as air.

But if we're not careful, even our digital lives can get cluttered. When we spend an hour searching our laptop for a "lost" file, important e-mail, or elusive bookmark, we become weighed down with frustration and lost productivity. Therefore, we should curate our digital assets as carefully as our physical ones. We should let go of the unnecessary, organize the keepers, and continually refine the content of our devices.

Unless we run out of hard-drive space, we rarely think of curating what's on our computers. But streamlining their contents can make for a smoother, more efficient experience. Digital documents become outdated just like physical ones do. Delete those that are no longer relevant to your life or business. Save only your best or most interesting photos instead of every shot you take. Get rid of browser bookmarks in which you no longer have any interest.

Cull these digital duds as you come across them, just as you'd put individual items in your Out Box. Additionally, set aside a day each year to do a full-scale purge. I recommend a digital declutter each January — it gives you a fresh start and renewed focus for the coming year.

It's also important to organize your digital stuff: Consolidate files, photos, bookmarks, and media into a well-ordered set of folders. Sort your documents by topic (financial, personal, work-related) and your photos by subject or date. Use subfolders to get more specific. Don't rely on your computer's search function; arrange things methodically, as you would in a physical file cabinet. Create a system that works for you, and make sure each kind of file you create or receive has a logical place to go.

Be particularly diligent with e-mail. Delete messages that are unimportant or that you're unlikely to read again; don't save every newsletter, promotion, or shipping notification you receive. For e-mails you've dealt with but want to keep, organize them into folders by subject or sender; they'll be easier to reference if needed. An empty inbox is a magical thing, something I achieve once in a blue moon but a worthy goal nonetheless.

Finally, refine your digital life as much as possible to minimize distractions. To lighten up your e-mail, unsubscribe from all but your favorite newsletters and mailing lists. Instead of letting bloggers or retailers clutter your inbox, go to their websites when you want to read or buy something. Slim down your social media accounts as well; better to live your life than share every detail about it. Remove most of the apps from your phone and disable notifications; seek out information when you need it, rather than dig through an avalanche for the occasional nugget.

No doubt about it, digital technology helps us reclaim our space. But when we lighten up our digital lives, we reclaim something just as precious — our time and attention.

towels

Towels may seem a trivial item, but they sure can take up space. They're big, bulky, and seem to multiply of their own accord. Corralling them on laundry day, and wrestling them in and out of a packed linen closet, can make for a long and frustrating chore.

Don't waste precious time managing an excess of towels; pare them down to just enough. They'll more easily move through your household—from shelf to rack to laundry and back—without any glut along the way. In living lightly, our goal is to create domestic routines that flow so smoothly, we barely give them a second thought.

To start, don't feel obligated to own towels in every conceivable size. Bath towels and hand towels will cover your needs and simplify things immensely.

If you want to live as minimally as possible, you can get by with one bath towel for each member of the household. Most people, however, will prefer two. Bath towels should generally be washed after three to four uses, so choose what makes sense for your laundry schedule. If you regularly have overnight guests, keep an extra or two on hand; that way, you won't have to scramble for clean towels the day of their arrival.

Here's a handy equation to determine what you need:

Towels = (Household members × 2) + (Max. number of overnight guests at one time)

Additionally, if you have children, pets, or potentially leaky pipes, save a few old towels for big messes. Use the ones that are too worn or shabby to hang in your bathroom. If possible, store them separately from your good towels, like in a basement or utility room.

Hand towels are used more frequently and should be changed daily. Keep seven per sink if you launder weekly (or fewer if you wash more often).

Don't feel the need to buy matching sets—that's how you end up with too many towels and sizes you don't use. A mismatched aesthetic adds personality to your bathroom, ease of replacement, and the opportunity for each family member to have their own color or pattern.

In addition to reducing your number of towels, lighten up the towels themselves. Flat woven towels like the Turkish *pestemal* are soft, lightweight, and absorbent, and take up just a quarter of the space of a traditional terry. They also dry more quickly, by both air and machine, making them more eco-friendly and less mildew-prone.

What to do with your excess? Donate new (or nice) ones to a homeless shelter and shabbier ones to a pet shelter. Let them go out in the world and do good rather than sit in your linen closet.

bedding

Maybe it's our nesting instinct, but many of us take a "more is better" approach to bedding. We're often reluctant to get rid of old sheets, blankets, and duvets when we replace them, and we inadvertently end up with a lifetime supply — or enough to host a giant sleepover.

The problem is, bedding takes up a lot of storage space. A lighter approach gives us much-needed breathing room.

Start with a Clean Slate by clearing out the closet, drawers, or other places where you keep your bedding. Then consolidate them into sets: a fitted sheet, flat sheet, and pillowcases for each bed in your home. When they're all jumbled together, it's impossible to tell which size is which, what goes with what, and just how many of each that you have. Fold each set into its own little bundle for a neater linen closet.

Choose your sheets wisely, and you won't need separate sets for summer and winter. Linen, for example, is a breathable fiber that's comfortable in every season. It's also durable, making for long-lasting bedding that gets softer over time. In fact, antique linen sheets (some over a hundred years old) are sought-after items at French flea markets. Simple cotton sheets can also work year-round.

Two sets per bed are sufficient for most households; that way, you have an extra when one's in the wash. If you have young children, it's prudent to have a few more on hand. Put the leftovers in your Out Box, and depending on their condition, pass them on to a local homeless or animal shelter. Henceforth, donate your old bedding whenever you buy something new.

For blankets, quilts, and duvets, make comfort your priority. Consider your climate, and opt for something that keeps you warm on those wintry nights. Just remember, you can only use so many at once. The number needed for family members (and a guest or two) at any one time is enough.

As for pillows, take the time and effort to find one that works for your sleep position (side, stomach, or back) and loft preference (soft, fluffy, flat, or firm). Strike the right balance, and instead of stacking multiples, you might get by with just one.

When it comes to bedding, focus on function not fashion. The more throw pillows, coverings, and fussy décor on your bed, the longer it takes to clear off each night and make up in the morning. Keep things simple, using the minimum you need for a good night's rest. The lighter your sleeping space, the more serene you'll feel.

books

As an avid reader and writer, I know it's tempting to give books a free pass. They're bulky, heavy, and hard to move, yet it's hard to imagine taking a "less is more" approach to literary material.

Take heart, my fellow bookworms. It's both possible and painless to lighten up your library. In fact, it's more invigorating to have a fresh collection of favorites than a pile of books you'll probably never read again.

As always, start with a Clean Slate and clear off that bookshelf. Then use the following criteria to decide whether to keep each tome or put it back in circulation.

First, *have you read it?* In an ideal world, we'd have unlimited time to curl up with our beloved books. In reality, few of us have that luxury. When our To Be Read pile towers high, it's time for some soul-searching. Don't keep that novel your sister recommended or that must-read business book if you're not truly enthused about it. If you don't intend to crack it open in the next few months, pass it along to someone who will.

Henceforth, limit the contents of your TBR stack to a certain number of books or what fits on a single shelf. If you acquire another before working your way through the backlog, give up an old one to make room for the new. E-books are the exception—feel free to pick up that discounted bestseller when you have the chance. It's a great format for your maybe-reads, as a few more kilobytes won't weigh you down.

Second, *will you read it again?* (Or did you have to blow the dust off it?) I can't stress this enough: You don't have to keep every book you've read. Instead, keep only those books you pick up and peruse regularly. A Lightly bookshelf is an active space, not an archival one. It's meant for the books that inspire, comfort, or otherwise delight you on an almost-daily basis.

Don't hold on to titles you've finished just to show off your literary cred. There's a lighter way to prove you're well-read: Post a "shelfie" to your Instagram account or other social media, and your friends will know that you've tackled the Russian classics or kept up with the latest bestsellers.

Third, *do you love it?* There's something to be said for sentimental (or simply beautiful) books. Just make sure they're special enough to be on your shelf, nightstand, or coffee table. Your novels from high school may not make the cut, but your grandmother's Bible, favorite artist's monograph, or Jane Austen box set might. Curate your books as carefully as the rest of your possessions, and keep only those that are useful, beautiful, or bring you joy.

When a paper copy isn't necessary or doesn't enhance your reading experience, opt for e-books. It's amazing to bring your entire collection on a plane ride or relocate without lugging boxes of books. You can indulge your every literary whim with zero concern for storage space. If you mindfully select your print books and go digital for the rest, you'll have a wonderful library without all the weight.

With

FREEDOM, BOOKS,

FLOWERS & THE MOON,

who could not be happy?

OSCAR WILDE

hobbies

When deciding which hobby supplies or sports equipment to keep, consider how often you engage in the activity. The frequency with which you pick up that tennis racket, calligraphy pen, or crochet needle spells the difference between a half-hearted pastime and a true passion.

Yes, I know—we're all short on time, and if we had the choice, we would spend our days on the golf course or in front of our pottery wheel. That's why I use a once-a-month guideline: If you're not making time for an activity at least that often, you might want to admit you're just not that into it.

And that's okay! Sometimes we accumulate the materials for something we think we'll love and then . . . eh. It fails to live up to our expectations, or we just don't enjoy it as much as we thought we would. We feel guilty for wasting our money, stash away the paraphernalia, and tell ourselves we'll do it someday "when we have more time."

Don't let these items weigh you down. You have permission to give up the equipment, the supplies, and the entire activity. Donate everything to a school or senior center, take a deep breath of relief, and free yourself to pursue something you love.

For those hobbies that pass the frequency test, select one or two you enjoy most. Instead of trying to master every craft or sport, focus your energy on a chosen few. You'll have the time to gain expertise, finish your projects, and come away with more satisfaction.

If possible, limit each activity's supplies to a single container. Buying stuff for a hobby is easier (and sometimes more fun) than actually doing it. When the container is full, challenge yourself to use up some of your current stash before adding more. Likewise, complete those half-done projects before starting new ones.

Invest in a small supply of high-quality materials rather than vast quantities of cheap ones. For example, use gemstone beads instead of plastic, natural yarn instead of synthetic, and professional grade paints, pencils, and paper. Better materials make for a better experience and better results. That alone can motivate you to practice your technique and improve your skills.

Finally, if you really want to lighten up, choose pursuits that require minimal equipment: Take up running, learn to draw, start a blog. If your hobby of choice calls for bulky apparatus, opt for access instead of ownership. Rent infrequently used sports equipment, and go to an open studio or maker space to express your creativity. It's a great way to try something new before committing your money and space to it.

sentimental items

We all keep some items for sentiment alone, because they remind us of a special person, place, or event. And that's perfectly fine, as long as these tokens of your past don't detract from your present.

Commemorate lightly, and preserve your memories with as little mass as possible. Your mementos should be like the precious items in a child's pocket, bringing you joy and comfort as you skip through life, not burdens you must forevermore drag around.

Heirlooms can make your life heavy. They remind you of loved ones (which is good), but they can also crowd your home, cramp your style, and keep you from moving on (which is not so good). Your home shouldn't be a memorial, nor should you forgo your dreams of moving overseas because you inherited your parents' dining set or baby grand piano.

Instead of holding on to large pieces of furniture, complete collections, or a person's entire estate, select something single and small. When it comes to memories, a tiny object has just as much power as a big one. So keep one teacup from a set of china, your favorite item from a collection, or your grandmother's thimble instead of her sewing machine. Alternatively, keep digital photos of your heirlooms instead of the objects themselves—it's a weightless way to reminisce.

If you're worried about inheriting a pile of stuff, now's the time for a gentle, heartfelt conversation with aging parents. Explain that you're living more lightly, and want to make sure their treasured possessions go to the right place. Involve siblings or other family members in the decision process so that heirlooms end up where they're most appreciated. If no takers are found, work together to find a charity that can benefit from your parents' generosity. In the worst-case scenario — you get stuck with everything — consider hiring professionals (like an estate liquidator or auctioneer) to help with the cleanout.

Be just as selective with the sentimental items *you've* accumulated, like souvenirs, trophies, school memorabilia, wedding mementos, and other tokens of the life you've lived. A small, well-edited collection is far more manageable and meaningful than boxes brimming with stuff. Select the most significant item from each special time in your life — like your bridal veil or senior yearbook — for preservation. Favor small items over large ones, and you may be able to fit everything in a single keepsake box.

Do the same for your children: Devote a container to each for their most precious keepsakes and creations. Refresh this collection as they grow so that by the time they're eighteen, you'll have a special piece or two from each year. As for the rest, make liberal use of technology. Scan or photograph all those crafts, drawings, and other miscellany you'd like to remember but don't want to store. This compact treasury of their younger years can be a special gift to them when they reach adulthood.

The best way to deal with sentimental things is to never let them settle in. It's much easier to part with that greeting card shortly after you receive it, or your child's baby blanket right after she outgrows it, than five, ten, or twenty years later. With that in mind, let things go while it's still easy. If it's too late for that, put sentimental items On Hold—it helps you detach from them psychologically while you decide how best to rehome them. Giving special pieces to a museum, a friend, even a stranger who will cherish them can bring much more happiness than stowing them away.

Going forward, think long and hard before adding to your sentimental stash. Instead of keeping that playbill, take a selfie at the theater; instead of buying that tourist trinket, journal or blog about your experience; instead of saving the whole newspaper, scan the article in which you were mentioned. Instead of piling on mementos with each passing year, find lighter ways to remember.

As you curate your sentimental stuff, keep this in mind: These objects are nice but not necessary to remember the special people, places, and times of your life. It's your memories, not the mementos, that are magical.

gifts

Think of gifts as having two parts: the object itself and the sentiment behind it (like gratitude, love, or friendship). The former can weigh us down, while the latter is light, lovely, and lifts our spirits.

The whole point of gift giving is the sentiment, while the object is merely a symbol. Therefore, if you don't find the object particularly useful, beautiful, or joyful, release the symbol from your home and keep the sentiment in your heart. In other words, you can let go of that itchy scarf or tacky trinket while still treasuring the thoughtfulness of the giver.

Don't keep items just because they were gifts; curate them as you would the rest of your possessions. The label "gift" confers no special status—the "gift" is all the feels behind it, which remain no matter what. Keep those items that merit keeping, but know that the gift (in its most meaningful sense) needs no physical form to endure.

Sometimes we hold on to gifts so we won't forget who gave us what. A better solution: snap a photo of the gift, name the file with the giver and date, and presto—it's documented and memorialized forever. Better yet, take a selfie with the gift, and send it to the giver to show your appreciation. Once the giving and thanking conclude, the item has fulfilled its purpose, and you can do with it as you please.

Henceforth, strive to give and receive lightly. If something must trade hands, make it as immaterial as possible (set an example as giver, and request the same as receiver). Consumables, for instance, take much of the weight out of gift-giving: a decadent dessert, bottle of wine, or artisan soap will be enjoyed without leaving a bit of clutter. Moreover, it's a luxury to which the giftee might not have treated themselves, making it all the more appreciated.

Experiences are even lighter. An art class, spa treatment, or tickets to the ballet make for a more enriching and memorable gift than anything bought in a store. The skills, well-being, or cultural value gained by the recipient can have a positively uplifting effect on their life. A gift of a charitable donation soars further still, spreading the goodwill of both parties to those in need—a magnanimous way to mark a special occasion.

For the most weightless experience, opt out of gift exchanges entirely. Let friends and family know you have everything you need, and prefer their presence over presents. Focus on spending time together rather than spending money on one another. Most of us would appreciate a birthday lunch with a friend far more than another possession.

Take the initiative to tell your friend, mother, sister, or colleagues that you'd like to celebrate more lightly; they may well respond with relief. If you throw a birthday party for your child, make it clear on the invitation that there will be "no gifts, just fun!" Let's be gift-free pioneers—the more mainstream the idea becomes, the less weight on all of us.

religion

Simplicity has long been considered a path to a more transcendent life. Through many of the world's religions runs a common thread: Earthly burdens like possessions, desires, and negative emotions are the source of our suffering. Whether symbolized by a heavy karma or the fall of Adam and Eve, this weight must be cast off for us to ascend into paradise or attain enlightenment.

For their part, the great spiritual leaders set wonderful examples of living lightly. Jesus, who owned little more than a robe and sandals, advised, "Sell what you have, and give to the poor, and you will have treasure in heaven" (Matthew 19:21, World English Bible). He invited all who were "heavy laden" to lighten their burden by following him. The prophet Muhammad is said to have lived with few material goods, patching his shoes, mending his clothes, and eating and sleeping on the floor. He taught that wealth comes not from riches but from contentment.

Indian prince Siddhārtha Gautama, the historical Buddha, renounced his worldly riches and said if we empty our proverbial boat, it may "go lightly" to Nirvana. Jain teacher Mahavira preached the virtue of *aparigraha,* or non-possessiveness, and Hindu leader Mahatma Gandhi died with fewer than ten earthly possessions. Nature-based faiths revere earth and all its life, and advocate living in harmony with the environment.

Of course, we don't need to don a habit to follow a more spiritual path; our capsule wardrobes will do just fine. When we live lightly, we can release earthly burdens and rediscover our ethereal nature—the divine essence (God, Tao, Dharmakaya, Brahman, Logos) that connects us to one another and the universe. Whether or not we follow a formal doctrine, there's bliss to be found in a lighter, less materialistic existence.

baby gear

Living lightly with children isn't always easy, but it's one of the greatest gifts we can give them.

Babies aren't born desiring stuff; they want love, comfort, and attention. The problem occurs when we use objects, instead of ourselves, to meet these needs. A hundred cuddles are far more satisfying (and space-saving) than a hundred stuffed toys.

But kids' stuff is so cute, it's easy to get carried away. We want to provide our children with everything (or everything we never had). And the gifts—oh, the gifts! All those little some-things add up, and our little ones end up with too much stuff before they blow out their first birthday candle.

If you're expecting (or recently gave birth), ignore all the "must-have" lists in magazines and registries. Acquire the bare necessities—like a crib, car seat, and clothing—but wait on the rest. Get to know your newborn before you invest in swings, play gyms, and the myriad other accessories for the under-one set. That year goes fast, and you won't need as much as you think you do.

If your nursery is already packed, pare down what you can. Put away anything that's not in active use; you can retrieve it later if you need it. (Put it in your Out Box if you think you never will.) Many baby items—wipe warmers, changing tables, fancy diaper bins—promise to make our lives more convenient but often just get in the way. Better to have a spacious nursery, where you can pace with a fussy baby without tripping over stuff.

In baby's first year, keep her clothing simple. Don't stock her closet with fancy outfits and frilly dresses. (You'll receive enough as gifts to use for photo ops and special occasions.) For the first few months, make a tiny capsule wardrobe of sleepers and onesies. Your infant will spend much of her time asleep. When she drifts off, the last thing you want to do is try to extract her from a pair of tiny jeans. As she learns to crawl and walk, add some soft shirts, pants, and leggings—they'll maximize her comfort and mobility.

Go light on the playthings as well—your infant will be perfectly content with a rattle and a few soft toys. Add basic developmental toys like blocks, stacking rings, and nesting cups as he gets older. Books, of course, are a baby essential: soft ones for him to hold, board books for you to read. It's never too early to start building your baby's library. Research shows that reading aloud to your infant from birth builds a strong foundation for later literacy success.

Overall, the less baby stuff you have to straighten up, sort out, and shuffle around, the better. In the sleepless haze of that first year, you'll need all the serenity you can get.

Despite what advertisers (and your children) tell you, more is not better when it comes to toys. In fact, a study published by researchers at the University of Toledo found that fewer toys make for calmer, more creative, more focused play.

Children benefit immensely from a serene and spacious environment. As parents, we want to provide ample items for our little ones' development, but we have equal responsibility to curate them mindfully. An excess of toys can leave kids distracted, overwhelmed, and ironically enough, bored. Rather than more things, we need to provide them with more room to play and opportunities to use their imagination.

Take a lighter approach to toys with a small selection of well-chosen, open-ended playthings. Instead of trendy electronics, opt for simple toys that encourage building, creativity, and pretend play, like blocks, books, animal figures, play food, crayons, dolls, and dress-up accessories. Avoid passive toys that require little more than pushing buttons; the more ways your child can play with an item, the better. Favor natural materials over plastic, and avoid mass-marketed "character" toys for as long as you can.

A broad guideline is to offer a half dozen choices at a time. Stash the rest, and rotate the offerings on a regular basis. Such a system keeps your child from becoming overwhelmed, and makes old toys seem new again when they reappear. If certain toys are continually ignored, lighten up by letting them go.

In fact, rather than buy more toys, create "invitations to play"—novel groupings of items your child can examine, explore, and experiment with however he likes. For example: a tray with paint, glue, buttons, and popsicle sticks, or a container with sand, pebbles, and pipe cleaners. Create them from whatever you have on hand: art supplies, household items, recyclables (boxes, fabric scraps, cardboard tubes), nature (flowers, pinecones, leaves), and toys (blocks, vehicles, figures). You'll find plenty of ideas online. Just remember to keep safety in mind, and include only items that are age-appropriate for your child.

Despite your best efforts, your children will still end up with toys of questionable value from gifts, goody bags, and giveaways at the dentist's office. If you're not keen on them, immediately put them On Hold and produce them only if requested. Unless they're particularly special, your child will likely forget about them, and you can send them on their way.

As your child grows, help her curate her own things. Teach her how to set limits on her possessions (like keeping only the plushies that fit in a basket), and encourage her to give up an old toy when getting a new one. Give her an active role in identifying outgrown items and donating them to children in need. Show your children how to live lightly early in life, and they'll have a wonderful philosophy to carry into adulthood.

Those who want
THE FEWEST THINGS
are nearest to the gods.

SOCRATES

décor

Decorative items aren't our most practical possessions—they don't keep us warm, make us dinner, or send our e-mails—but they fulfill a different and important need. They give us aesthetic pleasure, help us personalize our space, and remind us how lovely both nature and human creation can be.

The key to decorating lightly is white space—a generous amount of emptiness surrounding an object. If an item is worth keeping for beauty alone, give it the space it deserves. When you walk into a room with a dozen paintings, ceramics, or other *objets d'art,* you don't know where to focus your attention. In a room with just a few pieces, you immediately know what's special.

For this purpose, traditional Japanese homes have a small alcove called a *tokonoma*, used to display one or two decorative objects at a time. The chosen items reflect the season (like fall foliage or spring blossoms) and evoke an appreciation for both art and nature. Consider doing something similar. Designate a place to serve as your *tokonoma*—like a mantelpiece, console table, or small shelf—and choose its contents with similar care.

If you have more décor than can be displayed at once (and you don't want to part with it), tuck away the excess and rotate it seasonally. You'll always have a fresh look without acquiring anything more. If some items never make an appearance, put them in your Out Box and let them beautify someone else's home.

A rough guideline for a simple yet charming space is three decorative items per room. In the living room, that might be a painting on the wall, a bouquet on the mantel, and an artisan bowl on the coffee table. In the kitchen, it might be a candle on the windowsill, a vintage enamel pitcher, and a hand-printed tea towel. If you'd like a little more, display small groupings (a cluster of photos, a few bud vases or ceramics) instead of single items.

Remember, decorative items need not come from a store. The lightest, most ephemeral way to adorn your space is with nature. Nothing celebrates the season better than its bounty, like flowers, leaves, pumpkins, pebbles, stones, shells, and bowls of fruit. Best of all, they eliminate the need for mass-manufactured holiday décor you bring out only once a year. Pinecones and holly branches are prettier than plastic Santas and don't require any storage space because they can be composted when the season is over.

Finally, don't pack your home with designer goods because a magazine editor or online influencer deemed them chic. Your décor should reflect your own taste and experiences, like souvenirs from your travels, a meaningful piece of art, or a handmade item from a friend. Choose pieces that warm your heart, and you won't need many to make a beautiful home.

furniture

To lightly furnish your home, own just what you need, not what's expected. Never mind those magazine and catalog spreads. You don't have to have an entire suite of bedroom furniture if you find a nightstand, dresser, or vanity table unnecessary. You don't have to fill your living room with an oversized sectional if smaller seating is sufficient. You don't have to own a desk if you like to work at your kitchen table. You can leave your corners empty rather than fill them with chairs, tables, cabinets, or bookshelves.

Extra floor space is a wonderful thing! It makes your home feel larger and provides more room for activity. Instead of buying full sets of furniture, acquire single pieces as needed. Like dinnerware, your pieces don't have to match. In fact, your home will have more charm and personality if they don't. So take your time, and see if you can live without a console table before you commit to owning one.

For the lightest furniture footprint, choose multifunctional items like a sofa that doubles as a guest bed, a dining table that expands for a dinner party, an ottoman that hides your toddler's toys. Choose chairs you can shift around the house as needed, or a pair of end tables that can be used separately or combined for a larger surface.

If you move often, feel free to embrace the flat-pack life. Furniture that disassembles may not be the fanciest stuff around.

However, it's easier and less expensive to transport, making for smoother transitions when you relocate. Don't let an unwieldy living room set keep you from wandering as the wind blows. You can always invest in more permanent, heirloom-quality furnishings when you're ready to settle down.

Even then, remember that furniture is functional. Pieces that are overly precious or delicate weigh on your mind. Choose items that can hold up to kids, pets, and daily messes or that gain character with scratches, nicks, or wear. That white upholstery may be beautiful, but it's a burden if you're always worried about it.

To lighten up your furniture, identify the true workhorses in your home: the beds, the sofa, the dining and coffee tables. Those are your keepers. At the same time, notice pieces that aren't pulling their weight, in particular, those that do little more than collect clutter. If you don't have a table to catch your junk mail, it's more likely to go right into the recycling bin. In one fell swoop, you'll have a lighter, airier, more serene space.

lighten your step

Show your love to our planet by treading more lightly on it. Don't worry—you don't have to go off the grid or grow all your own food. The ideas here require little effort but have a lot of impact. Adopt a few of these eco-friendly habits, and see how easy it is to live in harmony with the earth.

waste less

When we walk through a beautiful park, we don't leave a trail of trash in our wake — dropping paper towels, plastic bags, and other detritus as we go along our way. Of course not! We take care to leave the grounds as pristine as we found them.

Unfortunately, we're not treating our planet as conscientiously. According to the Environmental Protection Agency, the average American produces 4.4 pounds of trash each day, or 1,606 pounds over the course of a year. Although a portion is recycled, most of it is incinerated or ends up in landfills. As we walk through life, we're each leaving behind a big pile of litter.

Instead, let's live more lightly on the earth and reduce our waste as much as we can. One of the most effective ways to do this is to eliminate disposable products from our households.

Both the making and discarding of consumer goods takes a toll on our planet; therefore, we want the stuff we buy to last as long as possible. Products used for just a few hours (or minutes!) hardly justify the resources and landfills they require. Give Mother Nature a little love, and do what you can to avoid them.

Instead of paper towels, use cloth to wipe up spills.

Instead of paper napkins, use linen. It makes for a more elegant and eco-friendly table setting.

Instead of accepting plastic bags, bring your own market tote to the grocery store.

Instead of paper plates or plastic utensils, use the real thing at your dinner table. Try bamboo, stainless steel, or enamel dishes for picnics and other outings.

Instead of making coffee with single-use pods, use a drip machine or pour-over setup. Instead of paper coffee filters, use a stainless steel one.

Instead of disposable diapers, use cloth. They're kinder to the environment and softer on your baby's bottom.

Instead of a throwaway razor, shave with an electric or safety razor (or a reusable one with replaceable blades).

Instead of paper giftwrap, use the Japanese *furoshiki* technique to fold your presents in a lovely piece of fabric.

Instead of drinking water from single-use bottles, fill a reusable one from the tap.

Instead of using foil or plastic wrap, pack your lunch in eco-friendly containers, like a bento box or reusable snack and sandwich bags.

The possibilities are practically endless. Consider reusable tea balls, silicone baking cups, refillable soap dispensers, reusable produce bags, rechargeable batteries, glass food storage containers, refillable pens and printer cartridges, wool dryer balls, handkerchiefs, stainless steel straws, and toothbrush handles with replaceable heads in lieu of disposables.

Furthermore, opt for items with minimal packaging. Avoid snack packs and products that are individually wrapped, and buy in bulk when you can. Support brands that don't encase their goods (like small electronics and cosmetics) in excessive amounts of plastic. Consolidate online orders so they can be shipped in a single box.

Finally, don't forget about food waste—all those groceries that expire or spoil before we get a chance to eat them. Each year, we discard millions of tons of food while millions of people go hungry. To cook and shop more lightly, prepare reasonable portions, and avoid economy sizes if you're unlikely to finish them. Compost as much of your food scraps as possible.

When aiming for less waste, awareness is the first step. To that end, make your kitchen trash can your only trash can. Remove bins from the office and bedrooms, and keep just a small bag in the bathroom cabinet. When you must walk your waste through the house to dispose of it, you'll become more mindful of how much you're generating.

- Pick a disposable item you use regularly, and replace it with a reusable version. Do you see a difference in the amount of waste you produce?

- See if you can make it a full week (or more) without emptying your trash can. Such a goal will inspire you to reuse, recycle, and compost everything possible.

- When you're about to purchase something, consider its eventual disposal. Will it (or its packaging) soon fill your bin? If so, seek a less wasteful alternative.

So

LIGHT A FOOT

ne'er hurts

the trodden flower.

WILLIAM SHAKESPEARE

eat lightly

Physiologically, we are one with the earth; we're made of the same elements and are completely interdependent. It's no wonder then that what's good for the earth is good for the body.

To eat lightly is to eat in a harmonious, rather than harmful, manner. Regard each meal as a wonderful chance to commune with nature. Be mindful of the food you consume — where it's from, how it's grown or raised, and its impact on the environment — and make choices that are healthy for you and the planet.

First, eat locally. Favor food that's grown in your community or region rather than halfway around the globe. Local food travels far fewer miles, requiring less energy to transport, process, and refrigerate. A shorter time from farm to table saves fuel, reduces emissions, and makes for fresher, tastier, more nutritious food.

What's more, eating locally preserves farmland and green space, preventing overdevelopment and sprawl in your area. And because small farmers plant a variety of crops — as opposed to the monoculture of factory farms — it promotes biodiversity in local agriculture.

Second, eat seasonally. In winter, don't buy tomatoes or blueberries from afar; they have a big carbon footprint and little taste. Buy your fruits and vegetables in season: corn in summer, apples in fall, oranges in winter, strawberries in spring. Consider joining a CSA (community-supported agriculture) program. For a fixed price, you'll receive a weekly basket of farm-fresh fare. It's a delightful way to eat! You'll become more in tune with nature and take new joy in its bounty.

Third, eat low on the food chain, meaning mostly plants. Livestock production pollutes the atmosphere and is terribly inefficient: It takes many pounds of grain (for animal feed) to produce one pound of meat. Given the enormous inputs of water, energy, and land required, it's far more eco-friendly to consume that grain directly.

To tread more lightly on the earth, eat less meat. Make it an occasional treat instead of a regular part of your menu. If you'd like, start slowly: Eliminate it from a meal or two each week while you experiment with vegetarian recipes ("Meatless Monday" is a popular strategy). For the meat you eat, seek out local, sustainably raised sources.

Fourth, eat organic. Synthetic pesticides and fertilizers use up fossil fuels, release greenhouse gases, and deplete the soil of essential microorganisms. They can also contaminate groundwater and pose serious health risks to humans. Organic farms use manure and compost as fertilizer, and natural forms of pest control—meaning healthier soil, water, and air and healthier food on your table.

Finally, eat less. Embrace the Japanese practice of *hara hachi bu*, a Confucian teaching that means eat until you are 80 percent full. In other words, stop eating when you're satisfied instead of when you're stuffed. Follow the example of the Okinawans — some of the healthiest and longest-lived people on earth — and recite *hara hachi bu* as a mantra before meals.

In particular, minimize the processed foods you eat. Avoid polluting your body with their preservatives and the planet with their packaging. Base your diet on whole foods — like fruits, vegetables, whole grains, nuts, and legumes — and limit everything else. You'll live lightly on the earth and love how light you feel.

↖ Try an "eat local" challenge: For one month, commit to eating food grown or raised within a certain distance of your home (like a 200-mile radius). It's a wonderful way to discover where your food comes from.

↖ Visit your local farmers' market, and become familiar with what's in season. Plan your menus accordingly, and make your meals a celebration of the current harvest.

↖ At your next meal, pause occasionally and notice how your stomach feels. Stop when you're no longer hungry, instead of continuing until your plate is clean or you can't eat another bite.

clean lightly

Cleaning should be like a dip in a mountain stream—pure, refreshing, and in harmony with nature.

Unfortunately, it's more often like a chemical bath: Many of the products we use to clean our bodies and homes are hazardous to our health and the earth. They contain toxic ingredients that can cause a range of ill effects, from skin and respiratory issues to chronic ailments. What's more, many of these compounds don't break down after going down the drain; they accumulate in waterways, harming aquatic life and contaminating water supplies.

Instead, let's clean lightly by using nontoxic, natural substances in both our beauty and housekeeping routines.

Seek organic alternatives to chemical-laden toiletries. For example, wash your face with honey. It tightens pores and moisturizes skin, and its antibacterial properties help treat acne. Simply wet your face, smooth on a teaspoon of raw, unprocessed honey, then rinse well. If you prefer a mask treatment, let it sit fifteen minutes before washing it off.

Oatmeal makes a good cleanser as well. Mix ground oats with warm water to form a paste. Rub it gently on your face and rinse, or let it dry first for a relaxing, spa-worthy facial. It removes oil and impurities, reduces irritation and inflammation, and restores your skin's moisture balance.

For a natural moisturizer, you can't beat olive oil. Use it on your face, in the bath, on your cuticles, and on dry or chapped lips. It also makes a wonderful makeup remover and hair conditioner. Be sure to use extra virgin olive oil, as lesser grades have been chemically processed.

And the list goes on . . . milk, yogurt, nuts, beans, oils, and herbs can replace the chemicals in your hygiene products. Look for items from green beauty brands or vendors at your local farmers' market. Alternatively, search the Internet for DIY recipes and have fun whipping up shampoos, body washes, and facial treatments with your favorite natural ingredients. For safety, patch test on a small area of skin and avoid substances to which you have allergies or sensitivities.

Now that we've detoxed our beauty routines, what about our homes? Can we really keep them sparkling without scary-sounding substances? You bet we can!

Baking soda to the rescue: It deodorizes, polishes, and removes stains without chemicals or fragrance. Add water to make a gently abrasive scouring powder that cleans pots and pans, sinks, tubs, countertops, and other surfaces. To neutralize odors, add it to your laundry, sprinkle it on carpet before vacuuming, or put an open container of it in your refrigerator.

White vinegar is another natural workhorse. Fill a spray bottle with equal parts vinegar and water to make an everyday, all-purpose, disinfecting cleaner. Use it on windows, stovetops, tubs, and tiles. It kills germs and bacteria and inhibits the growth of mold and mildew. It also removes stains and makes a great toilet bowl cleaner. Add a few drops of essential oil (like lavender or lemon) for a more pleasant scent.

And finally, use good old-fashioned Castile soap (like Dr. Bronner's) for almost everything: dishes, laundry, floors, surfaces, hands, face, body, and hair. For more all-natural ideas, consult the Internet or an organic housekeeping guide.

The key to cleaning lightly is cleaning often. Wiping down counters on a daily basis avoids the buildup of dirt and grime that might require stronger cleansers. Harsh ingredients that eliminate 99.9 percent of bacteria can do more harm than good, while a gentler hygiene routine helps preserve the beneficial microbes that enhance our health and immunity.

⚘ Read the labels on your moisturizer, soap, and shampoo. Do they contain substances you don't recognize or can't pronounce? If so, try a natural alternative.

⚘ For the next month, use a white vinegar and water solution instead of chemicals to clean your home. If you're happy with the results, make the switch permanent.

⚘ Would you like to purge your household of harmful chemicals? Call your local officials for advice on proper disposal, or keep an eye out for a hazardous waste collection event in your community. It's irresponsible and often illegal to put them in the trash or down the drain.

haiku

When life is weighing you down, read a few haiku. These delightful little poems can give you a new perspective on things, and (at least momentarily) make your worldly cares fall away.

In just a handful of words, they manage to convey deep meaning. What's more, they do so in a simple, graceful, almost effortless manner:

> *Along a mountain path*
> *Somehow sweet and charming—*
> *A violet in bloom.*
>
> Matsuo Basho, translated by William R. Nelson and Takafumi Saito

This sense of lightness (or *karumi*) was championed by Matsuo Basho, the seventeenth-century Japanese haiku master. He prized verse that was straightforward and unpretentious, free from artifice or elaborate styling.

So simple and lovely, haiku; but how can it help us live lightly?

First, it's a wonderful example of succinct and elegant expression. Each word is chosen carefully, with nothing extraneous.

We'd do well to choose our own words—not to mention our activities, commitments, and possessions—with the same mindfulness. In fact, Basho's life was as spare as his poetry: He gave up almost everything he owned in pursuit of his art, sometimes living in a simple hut, other times traveling throughout the country on foot.

Second, haiku connects us with nature. With its simple yet profound observations about blossoms, stars, trees, ponds, and earthly creatures, it reminds us of our place in the wider world and our unity with all creation. When you feel at one with the universe, you won't stress so much about that petty remark your colleague made or that designer handbag you can't afford.

Third, haiku helps us live in the moment. It brings our focus to the present, so we can release our hang-ups over the past and worries about the future. It's a Zen-like call to awareness, a reminder that if we pay attention to our everyday experiences, we can glimpse the true beauty and meaning of life.

buy less

Let's admit it: Many of the things we buy aren't exactly necessities. We purchase them because we saw them in an ad, because we want something new, because they're on sale — not because we need them. In fact, if we didn't purchase them, our lives probably wouldn't miss a beat.

What a great opportunity to lighten our consumption! All we have to do is resist these frivolous purchases, and we'll have more spacious homes, fuller wallets, and a healthier planet with nary an effort.

The first step is becoming aware of them. Can you remember what you bought yesterday, last week, or last month? We often shop spontaneously, making new acquisitions with little thought. These items then settle into our homes, and we pretty much forget about them.

To become more mindful of your purchases, track them. In other words, make a list of everything you buy. When you put it on paper, you can't forget about that impulse buy by hiding it in a closet. Review the list regularly, and make checkmarks next to the non-necessities — everything other than food, toiletries, and the basic clothing and housewares you absolutely need.

What do those checkmarks tell you? Do you tend to buy excessive clothes, shoes, tchotchkes, or craft supplies? Now you know where you can cut back.

To do so, try a no-shopping challenge. Restrict your purchases for a specific time period (like three months, six months, or a year). You can pick a troublesome category of items to avoid—such as clothes, home décor, or electronics—or refrain from buying anything other than essentials. For extra motivation, share your goal with friends, family, or on social media. The more people you tell about it, the more likely you'll stick to it. Perhaps you'll inspire someone else to buy less, too.

Also, don't let quantity discounts tempt you to buy more than you need. Avoid multi-packs, jumbo sets, savings bundles, and "buy one, get one" deals if a single item (or smaller amount) will do. That three-pack isn't a bargain if you just need one, and only leads to more clutter and waste.

Why is buying less so important? Because we share this planet and its precious resources with more than seven billion people. By consuming lightly, we conserve the earth's bounty for present and future generations. We take only what we need, so there's enough food, land, water, and energy for everyone. We don't make someone else suffer because we bought too much stuff.

Furthermore, when we buy less, we dispose of less, and that's always a good thing for the earth. Less consumption means less garbage to burn, put in landfills, and dump in the oceans, meaning cleaner air, clearer waterways, and a more beautiful planet.

When we're guests in someone's home, we don't ransack their drawers, eat the contents of their fridge, and leave mounds of garbage behind. We use only what's necessary and minimize our wear and tear. As guests on the earth, we need to act with similar respect. Don't let your eco-legacy be a pile of plastic, a clear-cut swath of forest, or more smog in the air. Buy less, and leave as little trace as possible.

- For the next month, keep a running list of every purchase you make both in stores and online. Review at the end of the month, and determine where you can reduce your consumption.

- What do you own too many of (T-shirts, cosmetics, kitchen tools)? Don't buy any more until you use up or wear out your current supply.

- Before you make a purchase, think "Lightly." Consider if you really need the item in question or if you can meet your needs some other way, like making do with something you already have or borrowing an item from a friend.

buy used

When you need to buy something, try to find it used. That's the most earth-friendly way to consume. By avoiding newly manufactured goods, you save energy and natural resources and keep perfectly good items out of a landfill. The longer an item can stay in circulation, the better, even if it changes hands several times along the way.

You can buy practically anything pre-owned, but let's focus on a few categories that can be particularly impactful in lightening your step.

Clothing is a great way to dip your toes in the secondhand market. Many people tire of their stuff long before it wears out, providing an abundant supply of lightly used clothes. In fact, you'll often find pieces that have never been worn. Shopping pre-owned is particularly savvy if you have children to outfit. Why buy something new when it will be outgrown so quickly?

Furniture is a big-ticket item with a big eco-footprint. Instead of splurging on new pieces, shop secondhand. With people relocating more often and moving costs so high, you'll find plenty of sofas, tables, desks, chairs, and bookcases looking for a new home. Give them shelter, and leave a few more trees standing.

Get your skis, bikes, elliptical trainers, and treadmills used as well. These items are usually perfectly fit for more use; by taking them over, you'll save a bundle of money and keep them out of the trash. If you need sports equipment for a child, look for a community exchange program; that way, you can swap your kids' outgrown hockey skates or ski boots for the next size up.

The same goes for lawnmowers, leaf blowers, garden equipment, and tools. Get them secondhand and keep them in service. They don't stay shiny and new for long anyway, and you can find brand names that are built to last.

And if you really want to lighten your carbon footprint, buy a used car instead of a new one. A huge amount of resources and energy is required to make an automobile. Sidestep this problem by acquiring someone else's. Opt for a fuel-efficient model; and before you buy, check the vehicle history report and go for a test drive.

Buying secondhand used to take a lot more effort than stopping by your favorite retailer; garage sales, flea markets, and consignment stores can be hit or miss. But luckily for us, online shopping has transformed the market for previously owned goods. With a simple search, you can find just about anything you're looking for in seconds; and it's just as easy to click the buy button on a used item as a new one. Websites such as eBay, Amazon, swap.com, thredup.com, and poshmark.com offer a wide selection of used goods and clothing, as well as a place to sell *your* stuff when you're done with it. If you prefer a local transaction, apps like Letgo and OfferUp connect you to buyers and sellers in your area.

In fact, the online secondhand market provides even more

variety than current retail offerings. It can be great fun to shop yesteryear's styles from your favorite brand or designer. If your beloved jeans have been discontinued, you may find a pair from someone else's closet. You might even score one new with tags!

- Are you currently shopping for something specific? Before you buy retail, check out consignment stores or garage sales, classifieds or Craigslist, eBay or other online sources. You may find a perfectly good, previously owned item.

- Make a pledge not to buy anything new for the next six months. It's a great way to discover all the marvelous goods available in the secondhand market.

- When you tire of your own things, don't throw them in the trash. Put them back in circulation. Resell them, repurpose them, or give them away for free.

How lovely goodness is
in those who,
STEPPING LIGHTLY,
go smiling
through the world.

VIRGINIA WOOLF

buy kindly

What if you could look into the eyes of the person who made the shirt you're wearing, the chair you're sitting on, the mug you're drinking from? You'd want to see satisfaction and happiness, not hardship or despair.

The things we buy don't magically appear on retailers' shelves. There's a backstory to every item, from clothing and kitchenware to furniture and office supplies, and if we're to live lightly, we need to learn more about it.

Before you make a purchase, question both its human and environmental impact. Consume with kindness by considering the following issues:

Who made this item? Were they treated humanely, paid a fair wage, and provided safe working conditions? Or did they labor long hours for low pay in a crowded sweatshop?

What is this item made of? Is it a natural material that's biodegradable? If so, was it sustainably grown and harvested? Or is it a synthetic substance whose production and disposal harm the environment?

How was this item made? Was it created by hand or in a factory? Does the manufacturer follow eco-friendly practices, or is it polluting the air and waterways in its community?

Yes, it's uncomfortable to think that another human being is suffering or an ecosystem is being destroyed so that we can buy a new sweater, but sadly, that's reality for many goods on the market. The tragedy is made even worse when we turn a blind eye to these issues and continue with consumption as usual.

This information isn't easy to obtain, but we should at least try. As a starting point, check the origin label. If the item comes from a country with lax labor or environmental regulations, dig a little deeper. Look into the brand or retailer's track record to find out if they're known for ethical sourcing, or have been repeatedly exposed for sweatshop labor or toxic pollution.

If an Internet search fails to bring up specifics, go straight to the source. Contact the retailer by phone, e-mail, or social media and ask, *Who makes your stuff and under what conditions?* To buy kindly, we must demand transparency in the supply chain. If their answer is unsatisfactory or your request is ignored, shop somewhere else. Better yet, let them know why; companies need to know that their customers care about these issues.

No doubt about it, buying kindly takes effort. You may discover that some of your favorite brands' practices leave much to be desired. But don't be discouraged. Look at it as an opportunity to support businesses that make the world better.

With a little research, you'll find companies deserving of your dollars: those who are committed to ethical and sustainable manufacturing, and who enrich and empower the communities in which they produce their goods. Moreover, online marketplaces make it a lot easier to buy directly from individual artisans. When you buy handmade, you'll bypass many of these concerns altogether.

Shopping ethically may cost a bit more, but when we purchase cheap goods, someone else is paying the price. Buying something should never do harm to the planet or another person.

We're often encouraged to "be the change" we wish to see in the world. When we vote with our wallets by supporting companies with good practices, we can "buy the change" we wish to see in the world, too.

- ⚑ Take an interest in where your stuff comes from. Before you make a purchase, look at the "Made in" label to determine its origin.

- ⚑ Start paying attention to news stories about manufacturing conditions around the world. Don't buy from countries or retailers who abuse the environment or their workers.

- ⚑ If you indulge in "fast fashion," educate yourself on how these cheap, trendy clothes impact the people who make them. (*The True Cost* is a wonderful documentary on the subject.) Consider kinder ways to shop for apparel.

buy for life

Imagine how satisfying it would be to have a dress that sees you through decades, a handbag for the long haul, a pan that's a treasured possession. It's a wonderful way to curate your life and live lightly on the earth. In fact, that's just what our great-grandparents did. Since consumer goods were scarce and costly, they prized quality and longevity. They expected their possessions to last their lifetime and to pass them down to the next generation.

Oh, how times have changed! In our modern era, stuff is cheap and plentiful, and styles change with the seasons. We shop based on price and trends rather than quality. (If that bargain jacket or toaster doesn't last the year, we'll just buy another one.)

But that's not living lightly. Every item we buy has an impact on the earth. Its production depletes natural resources, its distribution burns up energy, and its disposal clogs landfills. Each stage contributes pollution to the air, water, or soil.

To lighten our step, we should shop the way our ancestors did: buying things that will last, and that we'll want to keep, for a very long time.

What does buying for life look like? It's choosing a few pieces of well-made cookware over shoddy pots and pans you'll soon be replacing. It's buying a classic shift dress over a trendy outfit that'll be out of style next year. It's investing in appliances that can be repaired rather than those destined for the landfill.

First, look for durability. How can you tell if that hand mixer or sweater dress will go the distance? In some cases, you can use your instincts. If it looks cheap, feels cheap, and costs next to nothing, it's probably not going to last. But for the most part, you'll have to rely on reputation and product reviews. See if the item held up for others and if the company stands behind its products.

Better yet, seek out items with a lifetime guarantee. They might command a premium price, but if the manufacturer provides free repairs, they can be well worth it. You won't waste time and money buying replacements, and you'll keep a lot of junk out of the landfill.

Second, consider style. The ideal: one that's so timeless, you can't tell when it was made. Whether it's clothing, cutlery, or couches, the less dated, the better. Avoid the cheap and trendy items peddled by fast fashion, fast furniture, and fast décor retailers; not only are they shoddily made, they're quickly outmoded. If you stick to design classics, your stuff will never go out of vogue.

Third, choose versatility. We end up with multiples (and clutter) when we buy items with limited use, like novelty goods, specialty kitchen gadgets, or shoes that work with only one outfit. When our tastes or interests change, those items no longer meet our needs. Instead, opt for multipurpose products that will serve you well now and in the future.

Finally, keep your stuff going as long as possible. Give your possessions the care and maintenance they need to stay in tip-top shape. If something breaks, don't just give up on it—contact the manufacturer or take it to your local repair café, a free meeting place where volunteers help you fix your stuff.

When you buy for life, you buy with intention rather than on impulse. You set the bar high for things you bring home, and hold on to them for the duration.

- ⚘ What possession have you had the longest? Consider what makes it so special and how you might seek out these qualities in future purchases.

- ⚘ Determine which clothing styles suit you best, and instead of indulging in fashion trends, build a long-term capsule wardrobe around these favorites.

- ⚘ If there's a purchase on your horizon, take your time instead of rushing to buy. Research your options, and try to find something you might conceivably keep forever.

Heaven is
UNDER OUR FEET
as well as
over our heads.

HENRY DAVID THOREAU

Do you know what's a lighter, less stressful, more magical alternative to ownership? Access.

Oftentimes we need an item for just a short time, like a power tool for a renovation project or an evening dress for a black-tie event. Afterward, that circular saw ends up covered in dust in our basement, and that glamorous gown is consigned to the back of our closet. Which begs the question: Why spend money on and devote storage space to an object we might never use again?

To live lightly, access instead of acquire.

In our burgeoning sharing economy, we're moving away from the idea that we have to own everything we need. We're realizing that for many items, it's sufficient and actually preferable to simply have access to them.

The idea certainly isn't new. We've been borrowing seldom-used goods from our neighbors for centuries. In fact, community members probably shared more stuff a hundred years ago than they do today. What happened? Mass production made consumer goods cheap and accessible, so we ran to the store instead of next door.

But just because we can afford something doesn't mean buying it is the best use of our resources. And happily, technology now connects us to a plethora of goods and people who will lend them.

If you can't find what you need among friends, family, and

immediate neighbors, go online. Log on to your neighborhood forum, social network, or sharing app and post your request. Someone half a mile away—whom you might never have otherwise met—may be delighted to help you out.

Alternatively, go to the library—it's no longer just for books. Many communities have tool libraries, which give members access to home and garden equipment; maker spaces, with supplies for craft and DIY projects; and technology libraries, with computers, laser cutters, 3-D printers, and the like.

A Library of Things gives patrons access to an even wider spectrum of goods: board games, kitchen appliances, sewing machines, camping gear, musical instruments, children's toys, sports equipment, party supplies, and more. Some collections are housed in traditional libraries, while others are stand-alone outfits that charge a small membership or borrowing fee.

If you're unable to borrow what you need, you can likely find a more capitalist enterprise to rent it to you. While that'll cost some money, it's often still more economical than ownership. Plus, you won't have to worry about storing it when you're finished—making it a great option for bulky, expensive, occasionally used items. Rent tools from the hardware store, athletic and outdoor gear from sports and pro shops, photography equipment from camera stores, and formal wear from online or brick-and-mortar boutiques. If you seldom drive, consider joining a car share service and rent by the hour.

Access provides what you need without the headache of

ownership. You won't have to waste time and effort paying for, maintaining, repairing, insuring, and storing so much stuff. Even better, access saves our planet's resources from being wasted on rarely used items, lifting a tremendous burden from the earth.

- Before you buy a big-ticket item (a tuxedo, a snow blower, a second home), consider how often you'll use it. Would it be more economical to rent or borrow one?

- Seek out access options in your community. Is there a tool or technology center, a maker space, or a library that lends nontraditional items? When you know what resources are available, you'll be more likely to use them.

- Do you have stuff you're willing to share? Join a local network to lend things to your neighbors. You'll build community and goodwill, and you'll make some new friends.

ride lightly

For many of us, driving a car—which burns fossil fuels and emits carbon dioxide—is the largest component of our carbon footprint. Fortunately, we have many ways to ride more lightly on the earth.

First, explore public transit options. Is there a bus, train, or subway that can get you to your destination? By moving many passengers in fewer vehicles, public transit is significantly more energy efficient than car travel. It reduces road congestion and air pollution and can even decrease your stress; instead of fighting traffic, you can sit back, relax, and catch up on e-mail or a novel.

Consider carpooling with colleagues on your daily commute. Ask around at work to find a driving partner. Some companies help match riders based on routes and work schedules. Alternatively, use a ride share app to form a carpool group or schedule individual rides as you need them.

Even better, ask your employer if you can work from home. Telecommuting just one day a week can reduce your carbon footprint by 20 percent. Another option: inquire about a four-day schedule. Working ten-hour (rather than eight-hour) shifts will keep you off the road an entire day.

Is it possible to get where you're going by bike? Pedaling is better for the environment and your health. Plan your route carefully; instead of choosing the shortest one, consider variables like terrain and traffic to avoid steep hills and busy roads. For the safest and most pleasant experience, seek out greenways and bike lanes. You can find recommended routes on cycling and city transportation websites.

Walking is another gentle way to traverse the earth; do it whenever and wherever you can. It takes more time, but consider it an investment in your well-being: Walking helps you lose weight, lowers stress, and reduces the risk of heart attack, stroke, and disease.

If you must travel by car, drive a little more lightly to reduce your impact. Consolidate errands by going to the bank, dry cleaners, and grocery store in one trip. For better fuel economy, lighten your load by clearing out the junk in the trunk and removing the roof rack if you're not using it. Go light on the pedals as well. Instead of having a lead foot, start and stop gradually and maintain a constant speed. When it's time for replacement, opt for a more fuel-efficient car or an electric or hybrid model.

If you need a car only on occasion, choose a car share program over ownership. Cars are distributed throughout metro areas; when the need arises, simply locate and reserve one online, hop in, and drive away. Depending on the service, you can pay by the minute, hour, or day. "Free-floating" programs like ReachNow and car2go let you drop off the car anywhere in the operating area when you're done with it.

With a little creativity and planning, you can become a one-car (or car-free) household. If you can't do it where you live now, make it a priority for your next move and choose a location that's less car-dependent. Look for communities with greenways, sidewalks, and close proximity to shops and amenities. A neighborhood with a high Walk Score, Bike Score, or Transit Score can make your car-free dream come true.

- Check out the bus and train routes on your local transportation website. You may be surprised where you can go without driving. If you don't currently take public transit, be adventurous and ride it to work or some other destination one day.

- Become familiar with the sidewalks, bike paths, and greenways in your area. Challenge yourself to do at least one trip each week by bike or on foot.

- Make a list of your weekly errands. For those that involve driving, designate a particular day to do them all at once. Batching your errands saves time as well as gas.

peace pilgrim

When we live lightly, we gain the clarity to discover our true purpose in life. That in turn helps us live lighter still, as we pay far less mind to things that don't contribute to our calling.

There's no better example of this than Peace Pilgrim, a woman who on January 1, 1953, began walking "25,000 Miles on Foot for Peace" and didn't stop until her death twenty-eight years later, on her seventh time crossing the United States.

Her story is absolutely inspiring. After adopting a lifestyle of voluntary simplicity, she experienced a personal enlightenment: "All of a sudden I felt very uplifted, more uplifted than I had ever been. I remember I knew *timelessness* and *spacelessness* and *lightness*." She then conceived of her mission—to promote world peace by helping people find inner peace—to which she devoted the rest of her life.

She stripped away every burden in pursuit of her purpose.

She walked alone, without money, her only possessions the clothes on her back and the items in her pockets—a comb, toothbrush, pen, and some papers. She never asked for anything, and would simply walk until someone offered shelter, and fast until someone gave her food. What's more, she found immense joy in such simplicity: "There is nothing to tie me down. I am as free as a bird soaring in the sky."

Fortunately for us, her friends have preserved her teachings, conversations, and correspondence in the book *Peace Pilgrim: Her Life and Work in Her Own Words* (available for free at peacepilgrim.org). The story of her extraordinary journey, and the wisdom and clarity of her words, provide powerful inspiration for all of us to let go of what's unnecessary and focus on living our light.

dwell lightly

Generally speaking, the bigger your home, the bigger your carbon footprint. If you don't need all the space you have, dwell lightly by downsizing your digs.

Why should you love a smaller home? Let us count the ways . . .

A smaller home uses less energy, a boon to both the earth and your bank account. When you have less space to heat and cool, you'll reduce your electricity and fuel use, resulting in lower emissions and utility bills. Downsize enough and you may be able to power much of your home with sustainable alternatives like solar and wind. An apartment or condominium, insulated by surrounding units, can also be more energy efficient than a stand-alone dwelling.

A smaller home requires fewer resources (like lumber) to build and maintain. That saves trees and reduces the use of petroleum-based products like siding, insulation, and roof shingles. With fewer materials needed, you may be able to afford eco-friendly alternatives.

A smaller home takes less stuff to fill it up. When your space is limited, you won't need to buy as much furniture, décor, electronics, or even things like light bulbs. What a lovely gift to the earth! When you have smaller rooms, smaller closets, and smaller storage spaces, it's much easier to buy less simply because you don't have anywhere to put it.

A smaller home has less area to clean. That's fantastic if you'd like to spend less time on housework. It's also good for the earth, requiring fewer cleansers, chemicals, electricity, and water to keep things spic and span.

A smaller home allows for a smaller lot, which means less land given over to development and more green space preserved in your community. As a bonus, you won't need all the water, equipment (sprinkler system, leaf blowers), supplies (grass seed, fertilizer), and services (lawn mowing, landscaping) used to maintain large yards.

Smaller homes are commonly located in high-density neighborhoods, close to urban centers. That means better walkability, and access to public transit and bike lanes; you won't have to get in your car for every errand.

Finally, many smaller homes are older ones. When you buy a pre-owned house, you save resources and eliminate the waste involved in new construction. It's recycling on a grand scale.

A smaller home can have all sorts of positive effects on your life. Reducing your debt and living expenses makes for significantly less stress. You may be able to work fewer hours, spend more time with family, or choose a career based on your passion rather than the paycheck. What's good for the earth is good for you, too.

You don't need to live in a shoebox to live more lightly. The average American home is approximately 2,500 square feet; downsizing to half that is still a generous 1,250 square feet of living space. That's positively palatial compared to "tiny houses" and many urban apartments. With the right floor plan and some space-saving choices, like clever storage and multifunctional furniture, a cozy cottage can be more comfortable than a Mc-Mansion.

- Measure the square footage of your living space, or find it in your home appraisal or apartment listing. Knowing what you have now will give you a good feel for how low you can go.

- Are you using every square foot to its highest potential, or do you have rooms (dining room, guest room) that stay empty much of the time? Could you live without this "extra" space?

- For fun, browse some tiny home websites. Seeing how people (and families) live in four hundred square feet or less may give you a new perspective on your own space, or inspire you to seek something smaller.

lighten your stress

Take the drudgery out of your daily routine, and fill it with delight. In these pages, you'll cast off trivial tasks and digital distractions to focus on what really matters. A schedule with less busyness and more breathing room is a wonderful thing, enabling you to move through your days with poise, precision, and a new sense of purpose.

do less

The aim in living lightly isn't to get more done; it's to do less. That's the opposite of what we've come to expect in our fast-paced, hyperconnected world. In fact, sometimes it feels like we're all trying to outdo each other in how much we can fit into our days. When someone asks how we are, "busy" is often our default reply.

Every day we're under endless pressure to do it all. That was hard enough in simpler times, when "all" meant balancing a job and family. But the digital age — and social media in particular — has multiplied "all" a thousandfold.

In addition to our traditional responsibilities, we're now compelled to keep up with e-mail, post updates to social media, run a successful side business, build a personal brand, turn out stylish DIY projects, write a blog, change the world, and give a TedX talk about it. On top of that, we're expected to stay connected to friends, clients, colleagues, and strangers around the clock.

We're constantly reminded that there's *more* we could be doing, and that we can squeeze it into our jam-packed lives if we have the right apps, life hacks, or efficiency secrets.

Don't believe it. Despite what those productivity gurus tell you, nobody can do it all. *Give yourself permission to not even try.*

Ah . . . Doesn't that feel good? Just releasing that expectation makes you instantly feel lighter.

Instead of doing it all, curate what you'll do. Realize that time is your most precious commodity, and be highly selective in how you spend it.

First, curate the *number* of activities, projects, or commitments in which you're involved. Sure, it'd be wonderful to take an art class, practice yoga, join a book club, and learn to salsa dance; instead, participate in just one or two extracurriculars at a time. You'll be more likely to enjoy them and develop some expertise.

Similarly curate your community endeavors, like coaching Little League or helping at the pet shelter. The more focused your efforts, the greater impact you'll have. If possible, be selective with the projects you take on at work, and instead of automatically accepting every assignment, concentrate on a chosen few. Cap your social media obligations as well — the fewer, the better — to prevent distraction and digital burnout.

Next, curate your *time* and how you allocate it. For example, allot two nights a week to a specific hobby, one weekend a month to volunteering, or a limited number of hours to work meetings. Be particularly mindful of time sinks, like watching television, surfing the Internet, or browsing social media. Ten minutes here or thirty minutes there may seem trivial, but left unchecked can fritter away much of your day. Confine them to a reasonable time frame (like an hour per day) or a certain period (like over lunch).

Remember, the quality of what you do is far more important than the quantity. When you're stretched too thin, you can't devote more than minimal effort to your endeavors. When you have less to do, you can give full attention to the task at hand and perform at your highest potential. Doing less can mean the difference between mediocrity and mastery.

When you do less, you'll still have plenty on your plate, but you'll feel calm, in control, and capable of handling it. You'll glide through your tasks with the grace and precision of a figure skater, and finish each day feeling accomplished instead of exhausted.

⚑ Determine your favorite pastime and practice it exclusively for a month. Notice if it brings you more enjoyment and satisfaction when you devote your full energies to it.

⚑ Select the one philanthropic activity that makes your heart sing (like aiding the homeless or volunteering at your child's school). Figure out how you can further this cause with more focused attention.

⚑ Pick one or two social media platforms in which to participate, and ignore the rest for an entire month. Does paring down your distractions make you less stressed? If so, deactivate or delete the excess.

lightly decline

One day when my daughter was three, I asked her to do something that wasn't high on her priority list, like clean up her toys or finish her broccoli. She responded with a cheery "No, thank you!" and went on her way.

Accustomed to the brusque "No!" of toddler years, I was disarmed by the geniality of her response. I later found out she learned it in preschool, where the children were allowed to opt out of activities with a simple "No, thank you." It empowered them to make decisions and gave them a sense of control over their day.

My first thought: Wow! If only it were that easy for adults. My second: Why shouldn't it be? I vowed that the next time a request or commitment wasn't right for me, I'd lightly decline without a twinge of guilt. To my surprise, it worked.

None of us likes to say no. The word itself seems so harsh, so abrupt, so impersonal. It feels like we're rejecting not just the request but the person who made it. To make matters worse, we often load down our "no" with apologies, excuses, and long-winded explanations. By the time we're finished, both parties feel awful.

When we lightly decline, we take the weight out of "no" by saying it in the simplest, most gracious way possible. When you refuse a request, don't feel obligated to apologize profusely or make elaborate excuses. Believe it or not, a simple "I'd love to, but I'm overcommitted right now" will be understood and accepted by just about everyone.

While saying "no" feels like dropping a stone into someone's lap, lightly declining is a kinder, gentler way to give something a pass. It's more like a bubble, conveying its message and then evaporating into thin air.

Here's how to lightly decline with finesse:

1. Express gratitude for the request, admiration for their endeavor, or a desire to help:

   "Thank you for thinking of me . . ."

   "What a wonderful project . . ."

   "I wish I could help/attend/participate . . ."

2. Communicate that it just won't fit into your schedule:

   ". . . but my schedule is full at the moment."

   ". . . but I don't have the bandwidth right now."

   ". . . but this deserves more than I can give."

3. Finally (and optionally), wrap up with a helpful suggestion:

   "I know someone who would love this opportunity."

   "Can I connect you with [name]? This is right up her alley."

   "Here's a great resource you can use."

When you lightly decline, you focus on the positive. You make the asker feel good by communicating your support and enthusiasm for their work. You lend a spirit of goodwill (if not your time) to their project. Done properly, it avoids the guilt and disappointment that often accompanies "no."

And the best part of all? You're actually saying "yes." When you lightly decline a less important project, you say "yes" to more important ones. When you lightly decline a new commitment, you say "yes" to your current ones. When you lightly decline another demand on your time, you say "yes" to yourself and your loved ones. You say "yes" to taking control of your life and curating it with intention, saving your time and energy for what's most meaningful to you.

- Think of a common request you'd like to refuse (for example, "Can you help with this fund-raiser?"). Compose and rehearse a response so you'll be prepared when the time comes.

- If you have current requests waiting in your inbox, lightly decline them without delay. (If you didn't say "yes" right away, you probably shouldn't say "yes" at all.) Don't let these potential commitments hang over you any longer.

- The next time someone asks for your time, pause for a moment and think "Lightly" before answering. Will this responsibility weigh you down or lift you up? Answer accordingly.

What

SWEET DELIGHT

a quiet life affords.

WILLIAM DRUMMOND

unschedule

Think of the times in your life you've felt the lightest, the happiest, the most free. Whether childhood summers, your yearly vacation, or lazy Sunday mornings, they likely have one thing in common: They're unscheduled.

It's hard to feel calm when you live by the clock, yet the pressure to do so is relentless. Planners, calendars, and apps schedule our days down to the minute. Productivity experts tell us how to fit more into already full agendas.

Overscheduling is one of the most significant causes of stress in our lives. We rush from one commitment to the next, speeding through life on a strict timetable, ever fearful of falling behind. If our ten o'clock meeting or one o'clock appointment runs late, it throws the rest of our day into a tailspin.

To live more lightly, more serenely, unschedule your time. Instead of penciling something in, scribble something out. I know that's easier said than done, but start small. Choose a monthly or weekly obligation that's expendable, and see what life is like without it. Perhaps the world won't stop turning if you skip that working lunch or self-improvement workshop.

Build little buffers of breathing room between commitments. They give you a chance to pause and center yourself throughout the day. Feeling calm and in control boosts your confidence and performance, and having some breaks in your schedule keeps it from tumbling like dominoes if something goes amiss.

Don't feel guilty for having thirty minutes of free time before your next obligation. And by all means, don't be tempted to fill it! You're not making space in your schedule so you can squeeze in something else. You're making space so that instead of always doing, you can just be. In the midst of a busy day, a respite (however small) nourishes you physically and mentally so you can better complete your duties.

Unscheduled time is essential to your mental health and well-being; guard it like the treasure it is. Instead of agreeing to chair another committee, attend another meeting, or participate in another project, lightly decline: "I would love to, but I just don't have room in my schedule."

Life is no fun when it's divided into time slots. Enjoy the loveliness of having some empty space in your calendar; it opens up a wonderful sense of possibility. Rather than know everything you'll do in a day, leave room for a little serendipity — that chance meeting, unexpected event, or happy discovery that could never be planned.

When you're overscheduled, you hurtle through life like a train, so intent on reaching the next station on time, you miss much of the scenery. When you unschedule, you can flit through your day like a bird, accomplishing what needs to be done but pausing to perch, observe, and perhaps even whistle with joy along the way.

Life should be measured in moments, not minutes. When you're laughing with your child, chatting with your partner, or walking through the park, concentrate on the now—not on what you have to do next. Make room for these unscheduled moments, because they're what make life so delightful.

- Build an hour of unscheduled time into each day, whole or in thirty-minute increments. Use it to relax and refresh yourself however you see fit (take a walk, meditate, have a cup of tea).

- Remove a weekly obligation from your schedule. Instead of filling it with something else, embrace it as "found time" when it rolls around.

- Enjoy a completely unscheduled day (perhaps Saturday or Sunday) each week. Let your plans unfold naturally without concern for the clock.

stoicism

The idea of living lightly has roots in ancient philosophy, particularly Stoicism, a school of thought founded in third-century BCE Greece and later adopted and refined by the Romans. Though Stoicism's teachings encompassed logic, physics, and ethics, it was by and large a practical philosophy for living a good life.

Contrary to popular belief, the Stoics did not advocate suppressing emotions. Rather, they believed that negative feelings like anger, worry, and fear could be skillfully managed and minimized. They taught that our happiness depends entirely on our perspective of things. To put it simply, things aren't so bad when we don't let them upset us.

The Stoics were proponents of equanimity — maintaining an inner calm and evenness of mind, particularly in difficult situations. They recognized that life is full of change and uncertainty, and the best way to deal with it is to let go of things we can't control (like other people and external events) and focus on what we can (our reactions, opinions, and thoughts). Epictetus advised, "Seek not that the things which happen should happen as you wish; but wish the things which happen to be as they are, and you will have a tranquil flow of life."

And much like modern minimalists, the Stoics prized moderation and mastery over their desires. They weren't overly ascetic, but rather practiced a detachment to material goods and earthly pleasures—so as not to be overly concerned with obtaining them or upset in the event of losing them. They were grateful for what they had and recognized, in Marcus Aurelius's words, that "very little is needed to make a happy life."

For more inspiration, dip into some of the classics of Stoic philosophy, like Seneca's *On the Tranquility of the Mind*, Marcus Aurelius's *Meditations*, and Epictetus's *Enchiridion* and *Discourses*. Modern translations have made them delightfully readable and relevant.

unplug

Once upon a time, after we left work, we went off the clock until the following morning. Once upon a time, we had to be at home for someone to reach us by phone. Once upon a time, we had no idea what our friends were doing unless we ran into them. Once upon a time, we walked down the street, ate our lunch, and sat on the subway without staring at our phones.

Those were the days. Now we're expected to be reachable 24/7, keep up with acquaintances from twenty years ago, and follow the intimate details of other peoples' lives (or worse yet, share our own). We no longer feel comfortable sitting in a coffee shop or on a park bench and simply taking in the scene.

Being always connected has its upsides — a friend can text if she's running late, we can check the forecast while on the go — but the downsides are significant.

For one, the virtual noise is ceaseless, never giving us a moment's peace. Texts, calls, e-mails, feeds, headlines, and other distractions come in randomly, at all hours of the day, taking our attention from whatever we're doing. It's hard to work productively with constant interruptions.

Second, knowing what our friends (and strangers) are doing, wearing, eating, buying, and achieving is a recipe for dissatisfaction. Comparing our lives to theirs makes us feel less stylish, skilled, and successful. We're continually reminded of what we're *not* doing, and we develop a fear of missing out.

The noise, the pressure, and the expectations are additional burdens on our daily lives. Fortunately, lightening up is easy. You simply need to unplug.

The fastest way to serenity is to turn off notifications on your phone. Your life will be much more peaceful when apps, feeds, and news updates aren't constantly demanding your attention. Keep calls and texts on if you'd like, but switch off the alerts. You don't need to know the instant a store runs a promotion or an acquaintance updates her Facebook page.

You can similarly quiet your computer by turning off e-mail alerts. Imagine if every few minutes someone walked into your office and tapped you on the shoulder with a random question or request. You'd never get anything done! A nonstop stream of e-mails has the same effect. Designate a certain time that you'll check and answer messages, and ignore them the rest of the day.

Once you've experienced the bliss of a silent phone or laptop, consider unplugging entirely for part of your day, perhaps while eating lunch or after dinner. Turn off all electronic devices, and take a walk, talk to a friend, or pick up a book instead. Love the newfound peace and quiet? Try an unplugged weekend or vacation; it wasn't so long ago that it was the norm.

In days of yore, telephone cords clearly tethered us to the device (and whoever was on the other end). But today's wireless technology gives us only the illusion of freedom. We're now tethered—to work, advertisers, corporations, and more—by invisible cords that are far more insidious.

When you unplug, you throw off these virtual chains. *You* decide how to spend your time and attention instead of letting marketers, app developers, and social media companies decide for you. *You* take control of your day and free your mind for loftier, life-enhancing pursuits.

≮ Turn off (or at least silence) all nonessential notifications on your phone, and see if you feel calmer and more focused during the day.

≮ Experiment with being "unreachable" for certain periods of time. For example, reset colleagues' expectations by not answering work e-mails at night or on weekends.

≮ Ban all devices during meals and family time. Embrace the opportunity to gaze at your loved ones or out the window instead of at a screen.

stepping stones

Big projects can feel like big weights hanging over us. We're overwhelmed by the magnitude of the work, and instead of bouncing out of bed eager to tackle it, we drag ourselves to our desks with a feeling of dread. We don't know where to start, so we procrastinate, and as the deadline looms nearer and the work looms larger, our stress levels escalate.

Never fear. Not only can we live lightly, we can work lightly, too. We simply need to turn that big boulder of a project into smaller, more manageable stepping stones.

Imagine sitting down to write a novel—the enormity of the task is enough to paralyze the most seasoned writer. Sitting down to write a chapter is a little less intimidating, a single scene even more doable.

But what if you broke down that novel even more, and when you sat down to write, you aimed for just one paragraph at a time. Write a paragraph before your coffee break? No problem. Write another before lunch? With pleasure! Before you know it, you're stringing those paragraphs into a scene, a chapter, an entire book.

Stepping stones are a powerful strategy to increase productivity. Those small tasks are wonderfully easy to tackle, giving you a sense of accomplishment and building momentum toward completion.

This technique can be used for anything that feels intimidating, like learning to cook, code, or speak a foreign language. Break down the learning curve into mini lessons, and spend ten to fifteen minutes a day on a single skill. That way, instead of waiting until you have a large block of time to devote to it —which may never happen—you'll take a little step toward mastery each day. What's more, by lightening up the job, it'll feel fun instead of like a chore.

Do the same with goals. Often, these are so ambitious they seem unattainable. We can't imagine how to accomplish such big things in the small moments we have, so we fill them with distractions instead. That in turn leaves us heavy with disappointment that we're not making any progress.

Turn your big goal into mini goals: a string of smaller action items. It's daunting to try to "start your own business" in the hour you have after putting the kids to bed. But "brainstorm three ideas," "read an article on entrepreneurship," or "write an e-mail to a potential mentor" —that's doable. Create a series of stepping stones that keeps you moving along at a steady pace.

This strategy also gives you flexibility. Say your goal is a career change; rather than dive headlong into it (quitting your job and enrolling in graduate school), take small steps in the right direction (taking a night course, talking to professionals in the field). Each step gives you a chance to pause and evaluate, and the ability to change course easily if things don't go as planned.

Stepping stones are not just a catalyst for progress; they make heavy projects feel nearly weightless. Instead of buckling under a big load, you break it into bits and lay it at your feet. Buoyant and energized, you'll leap lightly from task to task, all the way through to the finish.

⚹ Select one of your goals and deconstruct it into the smallest steps possible — ideally, individual tasks that can be completed in an hour or less. Set aside a regular time to devote to them.

⚹ What new skill would you like to learn? Search online for mini-lessons in the form of short video tutorials. Plan a fun curriculum mastering the basics.

⚹ If you have a project that's stalled, think of a way to get it moving in a new direction. Try a small series of steps to see if the shift in path looks promising.

It is

TRANQUIL PEOPLE

who accomplish much.

safety nets

Do you know why trapeze artists can fly through the air with the greatest of ease, dazzling us with their grace, their courage, their weightlessness? Because they have safety nets. If we want to live lightly, freely, and to our greatest potential, we need a similar system to catch us if we fall.

Life is unpredictable. You may be cruising along smoothly when an unexpected turn of events turns your world upside down. Of course, you can't always prevent bad things from happening—but you can put safety nets in place to deal with them. They cushion your fall and help you bounce back quickly when something goes amiss.

But first things first: Pay attention to where trouble may be brewing. If you start suffering from mysterious aches and pains, your body may be sending a signal that illness is imminent. If your partner seems distant, your relationship may be faltering. If the atmosphere in your workplace becomes tense, a shakeup may be in the works. If you know where you're vulnerable, you can shore up your defenses.

In the best of scenarios, you can head off a potential problem before it becomes a full-blown crisis, like adopting a healthier lifestyle before you get sick, seeking counseling before your differences are irreconcilable, getting your résumé in order before you're laid off.

But sometimes, try as you might, it's not enough, and that's when a safety net saves the day. It's the health insurance that helps you get the treatment you need, the bank account that helps you leave a bad marriage, the professional network that helps you find a new job.

Building safety nets doesn't mean worrying about everything that could go wrong. It's simply creating a buffer in case something does. It's being proactive instead of reactive.

Safety nets range from small to big, so use them liberally across the spectrum. In everyday matters — having some emergency cash in your wallet or a backup source of child care — they can lower your stress. In extreme events — storing enough food, water, and supplies to weather a natural disaster — they can save your life.

When you have safety nets, you avoid becoming dependent on a particular person or situation. Appreciate the wonderful things in your life — like your job, your home, and your relationships — but realize that nothing is permanent. Set yourself up physically, psychologically, and financially so that a big loss won't completely ruin your life.

With strong safety nets — an emergency fund, a spiritual practice, a close network of friends and family — you can weather any crisis more lightly and gracefully. Once they're in place, continue to build and nurture them. The more robust and resilient they are, the better they'll serve you when needed.

What's more, safety nets empower us to rise to our potential. Few trapeze artists would step off that platform without their assurance below. So it is with us; we live more timidly, closer to the ground, when one false move could spell disaster. Safety nets give us the confidence to take risks, reach higher, make that flying leap of faith without the fear of falling.

- Take stock of your personal safety nets.
    - **Financial:** Do you have an emergency fund and insurance to protect your major assets?
    - **Professional:** Do you have a network of colleagues and employment options?
    - **Medical:** Do you have health insurance for both preventative care and in case of an accident or serious diagnosis?
    - **Social:** Do you have strong ties with family, friends, a church, or community?

- Take measures to fill any gaps. For example, research insurance plans, start a savings account to handle unexpected expenses, build and strengthen personal relationships.

- What risk would you love to take, and what kind of safety net might help you go for it?

choreograph

Even as we strive to do less, there are some things we just have to do. The house isn't going to clean itself, dinner isn't going to cook itself, e-mails aren't going to answer themselves (at least not yet). Sometimes we feel so bogged down with mundane tasks, we can barely accomplish anything else.

Not to worry! To get things done with minimal time and effort, we need just a few routines. Sounds boring, I know. But I like to think of them as ballet routines — a choreographed set of moves I know so well that I can perform them with precision, grace, and ease.

Take cooking, for example. If you take pleasure in it, devote as much time and creativity to it as you'd like. But for many of us, getting a healthy meal on the table after a long workday (particularly when we have kids to feed) can be the source of much stress. Having a routine — at least on weekdays — prevents panicking in front of a half-empty fridge or making a last-minute dash to the store.

To choreograph your cooking, develop a standard repertoire of easy-to-make dishes — like pasta, chicken, tofu, and fish — and change the sauces and spices for variety. A simple meal of steamed tofu and vegetables, for example, can be topped with a curry, peanut, black bean, sweet and sour, or ginger and garlic sauce. The possibilities are endless, and the process quite efficient. Instead of attempting a new recipe from scratch, you simply cook your standard dish and vary the topping. You can then save your culinary experiments for the weekend. *(Pirouette and plié . . .)*

Choreograph other household tasks, as well. Assign weekly chores to certain days of the week, like vacuuming on Monday, laundering on Tuesday, bathroom cleaning on Wednesday, and so on. That way, you can take care of them in fifteen-minute bursts, and avoid the disheartening prospect of spending your entire Saturday catching up on the housework. If possible, distribute tasks among family members. When the burden is shared, everyone carries a lighter load. *(Arabesque . . .)*

Routines also help with the more repetitive, uninspiring aspects of your job. To make them as painless as possible, devise templates for all those reports, spreadsheets, e-mails, and other documents you create on a regular basis. By standardizing the language and format, all you need to do is drop in the appropriate data for the situation. *(Relevé . . .)*

Better yet, automate what you can. If you regularly restock certain items (like personal care or office supplies), sign up for an online subscription program that delivers them to your door. Pay your bills online, and arrange to have recurring ones (like mortgage and utilities) debited directly from your bank account. Set up your computer to make automatic backups to the cloud and perform repetitive tasks (like resizing images or sorting files).

Use mobile apps to download coupons and send you event reminders, and employ a content aggregator to automatically pull headlines, articles, and blogs into a customized feed. You might even consider hiring a virtual assistant for tasks that need a human touch. *(Grand jeté!)*

With the right choreography, your work will flow like a polished and elegant ballet. You'll dance lightly through your daily tasks, saving time and energy for greater endeavors.

⚹ Which household chore do you dread the most? Choreograph a routine to complete it more swiftly and effortlessly.

⚹ Which work-related task takes too much of your time? Brainstorm a way to automate or otherwise streamline it.

⚹ With which job could you use a little help? Invite a partner for a *pas de deux*.

GRACE
was in all her steps.

JOHN MILTON

perfectly good

Remember when, as a child, you were given paints and a blank canvas? You'd happily dive into the task, delighting in the colors, the textures, the brushstrokes; and in short order, you'd create a "masterpiece." Imagine the same situation today. Would you approach it with similar gusto? Or would you freeze, paralyzed by the pressure to turn out something perfect?

Perfection — it sounds so lovely, but adds so much weight to our shoulders. Whether we feel compelled to write the perfect memo, cook the perfect dinner, or find the perfect gift, it makes the task heavier than it needs to be (and often sucks the pleasure right out of it).

Let's do things more lightly, and instead of perfect, aim for perfectly good. Sure, if we're proofreading or performing surgery, perfection is a worthy goal. But in most of what we do, it's not necessary or expected. So we're knocking ourselves out, improving and refining to make everything just so, and nobody cares.

Of course, we should always take pride in our work and put forth our best effort. But once our results are respectable, there's often little point in pushing further toward perfection. The extra time and effort brings much stress and little reward.

In fact, sometimes our quest for perfection can be downright debilitating. We set the bar so high, we feel incapable of achieving it. We worry that we're not talented, skilled, or creative enough, and we become completely intimidated by the task at hand. Instead of jumping in with enthusiasm, we procrastinate, leaving us with even less time to do a good job. Worst case, we don't accomplish anything at all.

When we embrace perfectly good, we're more enthusiastic to take on challenges. We feel confident that we can probably do an acceptable (if not flawless) job, and that's okay. Instead of fretting over trivial details, we get our stuff done faster and with greater ease.

In recent years, social media has raised the bar of personal perfection considerably. Our point of comparison is no longer our family, neighbors, and friends, but practically the whole world. And it seems like everyone is baking perfect cakes, wearing perfect ensembles, perfectly parenting their kids, and taking perfect photos to prove it.

What we don't see in those carefully curated images is the effort that went into staging them or the imperfection surrounding them. Pan out from that perfect soufflé and see the three collapsed ones behind it. Zoom back from that perfect closet and see the heap of clothes on the floor. Perfection can be styled, but rarely sustained.

When we aim for perfectly good, we cast off those unrealistic expectations. We realize that our family doesn't expect a photogenic dinner, our boss prefers a timely report over a meticulous one, and our kids would rather have our attention than an impeccable home. We can actually relax and enjoy life, rather than worry if it measures up to some lofty standard.

We can approach our tasks, our projects, all our pursuits with the exuberance we had as children. Freed from the weight of perfection, we can pick up our paintbrush with joy.

⚹ Think of one task in which you can give up perfection. Experiment with perfectly good for a month, and see if anyone notices a difference.

⚹ Has perfection stopped you from trying something new or challenging? Give it a whirl without worrying about the outcome.

⚹ Do you expect perfection from others? Consider some ways you can accept perfectly good from your partner, your children, and your colleagues.

lighten success

Much of our stress comes from chasing traditional benchmarks of success, like a big house, a fancy car, or another promotion. We struggle endlessly to achieve them, but even when we do, we feel unfulfilled. Why? Because they're usually *someone else's* idea of success.

What's more, conventional forms of success saddle us with additional baggage. That big house comes with a bigger mortgage, bigger property taxes, and bigger rooms to fill with furniture. That fancy car comes with fancy insurance rates and maintenance costs. That promotion comes with more stress, more pressure, and more hours at work. We thought "success" would make life easier, but instead it's made it heavier.

The solution: Define your own lighter, kinder, gentler version of success. Spend some time thinking about what kind of job, home, and lifestyle would truly make you happy.

Instead of a palatial house, it may be a modest one that's easier to clean, maintain, and furnish. You may prefer a friendly, walkable neighborhood to a ritzy gated community. You might want an apartment or condo so you can spend your weekends out on the town instead of mowing the lawn.

Instead of a car, you may get more joy from commuting by bike or on foot. You might find a car share or public transit more palatable than the oil changes, repair issues, and parking headaches that auto ownership brings.

Instead of a promotion, you may prize a better work-life balance. You might favor a flexible schedule over an impressive title, so instead of working longer days, you can be home to meet your child at the bus stop. Your idea of career success may not be landing a top executive position, but paying the bills doing work you love.

Your new and improved definition of success can be anything you want, like being a good parent, helping others, taking pride in your work, improving your community, or maintaining your health. Such goals are not only more attainable; if they align with your values, they're much more satisfying.

Furthermore, make your own measures of success instead of looking externally for them. Success shouldn't be gauged by your salary or bank account, nor should it be measured by social media. Success has nothing to do with the number of "friends," followers, or likes you have; in fact, the time spent pursuing such metrics can prevent you from accomplishing something that actually matters.

Finally, let go of the idea that to be successful, you must live an extraordinary life. Stories of people making fortunes with side hustles, writing breakout bestsellers, or otherwise achieving against all odds — and how you can, too! — dominate our news feeds. In our information age, these anecdotes are everywhere, making extraordinary feel like something to which we all should aspire. Realize they're more the exception than the rule, and that an "ordinary" life of kindness, well-being, and service to others is every bit as successful.

Success by society's standards is like a giant trophy: big and shiny but a pain to lug around. It's impressive to others, but can be oppressive to you. Instead, opt for your own version of success—a lighter, more uplifting one that makes you feel like a million bucks.

- If any of your "successes" (big house, high-pressure job) are weighing you down, consider ways you can trade them for something lighter.

- Determine *your* sweet spot of success—in other words, the circumstances that would make you happiest (like working for yourself or living in a walkable town). Devise an action plan to achieve it.

- In what "ordinary" way (kindness, honesty, generosity, family) can you be wildly successful?

effortless action

When we live lightly, something amazing happens: Released of our burdens, life becomes less of a struggle. We're able to do what we do with a new sense of lightness. We move, speak, work, and play in an easy, graceful manner that comes as naturally as breathing.

This state of effortless action is known as *wu wei*. It's one of the most important concepts in the *Tao-te Ching*, Lao-tzu's ancient Chinese manual for living. *Wu wei* means to act without acting or do without doing. It sounds paradoxical, but it means that instead of trying too hard, you let your actions flow.

Such lightness of doing is brilliantly illustrated in a short story by Italo Calvino, "The Adventure of a Skier." It takes place on a crowded ski slope, where a group of brash and clumsy boys are enchanted by the elegant, efficient moves of a girl in a sky blue parka: "They wouldn't have been able to explain why, but this was what held them spellbound: all her movements were as simple as possible and perfectly suited to her person; she never exaggerated by a centimeter, never showed a hint of agitation or effort, or determination to do a thing at all costs, but did it naturally."

As the boys tumbled noisily and awkwardly down the mountain, they watched her glide by with an unhurried, serene precision: "There, in the shapeless jumble of life, was hidden the secret line, the harmony, traceable only to the sky-blue girl, and this was the miracle of her, that at every instant in the chaos of innumerable possible movements she chose the only one that was right and clear and light and necessary, the only gesture that, among an infinity of wasted gestures, counted."

When we stop forcing our actions, we can do things with focus, with flow, and without exertion — as if we were born to do whatever we're doing. It's not a matter of striving, but of lightening up and letting go. Then we, too, can move through life as naturally, as expertly, and as gracefully as the sky-blue girl.

live your light

All of us have a light inside—a spark that's ignited when we discover our true purpose in life. In the simplest terms possible, it's what makes life worth living.

If you haven't found yours yet, living more lightly can help. Eliminating the excess from your life brings a wonderful clarity. Once the distractions are gone, you're better able to see what's truly important to you. It's amazing how your purpose materializes once you've made some space and time for it.

Your light can be anything: championing a cause, working toward a cure, beautifying the world with your art, being the best parent you can be. Typically its benefits reach beyond yourself, making the world, or someone else's life, brighter for having you in it.

Once you discover your light, focus all of your energy on living it. Use it as a filter for everything you do: Does this activity help me live my light? Whether you're about to read an article, join a committee, or begin a project, first consider if it furthers your grand mission in life. Eliminate those tasks and commitments that don't, and embrace those that do.

When you try to do everything, your efforts are directionless; they dissipate quickly and have little impact. But when you direct your energy toward a single pursuit—the one that stirs your soul—your potential for achievement is limitless.

Most of us spend our lives doing what we think we should

do, or what others (parents, partners, employers) tell us to do. When you live your light, you spend your life doing what you're *meant* to do rather than what you're expected to do.

Finding and following your calling is a big deal, but it makes life infinitely lighter. Suddenly, what you need to do each day—and what you don't—becomes crystal clear. You can easily say no to things that don't contribute to your cause. Instead of doing a million trivial tasks, you concentrate on the few important ones.

What's more, when your life has direction, you no longer need distraction. Television, shopping, social media, celebrity gossip, and other idle entertainment become altogether less appealing, as they have little to lend to your cause. Your priorities shift from consumption to creation, resulting in a greater sense of fulfillment and satisfaction.

So what of your day job and everyday chores? They, too, serve your greater purpose. A roof over your head, a clean environment, and food on your plate are essential for your well-being, keeping you safe and healthy enough to accomplish your ultimate goal.

That said, consider ways you can align your career with your calling. Perhaps you can shift focus in your field or use your professional skills in a philanthropic capacity. In the best-case scenario, you can make a living while making a difference. Spending your days doing meaningful work is the holy grail of happiness.

Your light gives meaning to your life. Instead of just going through the motions, you'll have *reason* for what you do. You'll see each day as a gift, another glorious twenty-four hours to pursue your passion. When your thoughts, your actions, your very being resonate with such purpose, you'll feel positively radiant.

- ⚹ What lights you up? Whether it's making music, practicing medicine, or volunteering, consider how this passion brings joy, peace, help, beauty, or kindness to others.

- ⚹ If certain activities and commitments take time away from your light, plan how to reduce or eliminate them.

- ⚹ Does your current job help you live your light? If not, think of some steps you can take—a different position, a shift in responsibilities, a career change—to make work more fulfilling.

lighten your spirit

Lift the weights from your heart, and move through life with more mindfulness. The advice herein will help you transcend your ego and manage your emotions with equanimity and grace. You'll learn to feel lightly, act kindly, and perhaps even find a deeper connection with the universe.

How did life become so heavy? Suddenly we have five more projects on our plate, ten more pounds on our body, and a million more things on our mind—and no idea how it happened.

Here's how: We sped through our days without paying attention.

To live lightly, we need to stop, slow down, and savor life. We need to live more mindfully, being fully aware and present in every moment.

When we eat mindlessly—distracting ourselves with television or the Internet, or simply being lost in thought—our meals fail to satisfy us. We eat more and gain extra weight on our body.

By the same token, when we live mindlessly—too busy to focus on what we're seeing, hearing, thinking, or feeling—our days fail to satisfy us. We do more, buy more, consume more information, and gain extra weight in our life.

When we practice mindfulness, on the other hand, we relish every aspect of our day and feel satiated by it. Not only do we not need anything more, we don't have the time or desire for it.

When we savor our food, for example, we eat with less distraction and more appreciation. We chew slowly and think about the flavors, the textures, and the nourishment it provides our body. We give our stomach a chance to catch up and feel full. Hence, we can eat more lightly.

When we savor our possessions, we appreciate the coziness of our sweater, the versatility of our smartphone, the comfort of our sofa. We treasure what we already own and don't feel the need to replace, upgrade, or add to our material things. Hence, we can consume more lightly.

When we savor our work, we focus on its quality and the contribution it makes to our company or society. We don't mindlessly opt for quantity, taking on extra tasks or responsibilities to prove our worth. Hence, we can work more lightly.

When we savor our leisure time, we delight in our children's play, our partner's conversation, a rambling walk through the woods. We don't fill our minutes and minds with pointless TV shows, tabloid news, or social media feeds. Hence, we can play more lightly.

When we savor our emotions, we take the time to recognize them, understand them, and do what we must to address them. We don't ignore them, fixate on them, or rely on vices or distractions to cover them up. Hence, we can feel more lightly.

Not sure where to start? Close your laptop while you eat your lunch. Take off the headphones on your daily walk. Turn off the phone when you play with your children. Work with focus and without scrolling news feeds. Savoring is not an extra thing to do; it's doing what you do with more presence.

When we savor, we not only take the weight off our own shoulders, we lessen the burden on all of society. If more of us eat mindfully, we'll have less obesity and lower health-care costs. If more of us consume mindfully, we'll have fewer environmental ills. If more of us live mindfully, we'll feel more peaceful and connected to each other and the world around us.

I promise you this: Once you learn to savor, you'll never want for more.

- Savor every bite of a meal today. Eat slowly, and appreciate the color, aroma, and flavor of your food. Think of the farmer who grew or raised it, the earth, sunshine, and rain that made it possible. Do you feel more satiated when you're finished?

- Take a walk around your block and focus on every detail along the way—the sights, sounds, smells, even the feel of the air (crisp, humid, breezy). Perhaps you'll discover something you've never noticed before.

- Savor a conversation with your partner, child, or friend. Maintain eye contact, and really listen to what they're saying (instead of checking your phone or letting your thoughts wander). Note how it feels to be fully present with them.

sophrosyne

I'll tell you the secret to living lightly but splendidly: *sophrosyne*. Not to worry if you've never heard the word before. *Sophrosyne* is the ancient Greek virtue of taking joy in a temperate way of life. In essence, it's a lovelier, more expansive version of moderation.

A thorough understanding of the term requires a reading of Plato's *Charmides* and *The Republic,* but I'll give you my interpretation and tell you how it can help us live more lightly.

As I see it, *sophrosyne* has three main facets: mindfulness, self-control, and harmony.

Many of us run into trouble with "moderation" because the concept itself is so vague. It's tempting to give ourselves a lot of leeway and say moderation is eating half the bag of chips instead of the whole thing. Moderation is the self-control part of *sophrosyne,* but oftentimes it feels like self-denial.

That's where *sophrosyne* shines. Adding mindfulness and harmony to self-control makes moderation more doable and delightful.

Mindfulness takes the guesswork out of moderation by making it personal: It's knowing when *you've* had enough. Instead of mindlessly eating the bag of chips, you realize that your craving is satisfied with a handful, and you don't need any more. It's recognizing where you tend to overindulge—eating too much sugar, buying too much stuff, watching too much TV—so you can be vigilant before veering into excess.

Self-control is stopping at enough. While mindfulness is *knowing* when to stop, self-control is actually doing it. It's controlling your desires instead of letting them control you. It's a wonderful skill to develop, but in the beginning it helps to limit access to things you can't resist. For example, if you're trying to eat sweets in moderation, don't keep any in the house. Indulge only when you go to a bakery or restaurant. That way, you won't constantly have to fight temptation.

Harmony is being happy with enough. Instead of feeling deprived when practicing moderation, you feel balanced and satisfied. You take more pleasure, for instance, in saving space or money than in acquiring more possessions.

Sophrosyne, then, isn't feeling sad because you "can't" have a donut for breakfast; it's eating a healthy diet because it makes you feel great.

Sophrosyne isn't yearning for some fashion blogger's trendy outfit; it's loving your small capsule wardrobe and plentiful closet space.

Sophrosyne isn't turning off the TV reluctantly but being thrilled to have extra time for the activities you love.

Sophrosyne isn't agonizing over every item you declutter; it's releasing your excess with a sigh of relief.

Sophrosyne isn't choosing moderation because you *should*, but because it gives you a deep sense of joy and contentment.

Practicing *sophrosyne* is like being a finely tuned instrument, with all your thoughts, values, and actions aligned. What's more, like the melodious note from a plucked string, *sophrosyne* radiates out to the rest of the world, helping you live in harmony with nature and everyone else.

Too much of a good thing can weigh you down—with pounds, with debt, sometimes even with addiction. *Sophrosyne* is just enough of a good thing. It gives you pleasure and satisfaction while keeping your life, your body, and your spirit light.

- ✎ Be mindful of where you overindulge and when you've crossed from enough into excess (like five cookies or three hours of binge-watching).

- ✎ Make a plan to enjoy your guilty pleasures more moderately (limit sweets to the weekends, web surfing to an hour, alcohol to a single serving).

- ✎ Contemplate some other ways in which practicing *sophrosyne* can make you healthier, happier, or more financially sound.

zen

If there's any philosophy that espouses a lightness of being, it's Zen Buddhism. Zen encourages us to let go—of thoughts, desires, possessions, expectations, and any kind of attachment—so that we may overcome the trials and tribulations of a material life.

Zen teaches that everything is impermanent, and that we should embrace change rather than cling to the way things are, or the way we wish they would be. At its core is the magnificent and paradoxical potential of emptiness: that once everything falls away, everything is possible.

Zen is free of dogma and ritual and is centered on *zazen* —the act of sitting in stillness to reach a state of enlightenment. Meditation helps us quiet the mind and focus on the present, so that we may realize our essential nature and oneness with the universe.

The goal is not to escape life, but to bring this heightened awareness into our daily routines: "When walking, walk; when eating, eat." We just need to live mindfully, in the moment, even while doing mundane things. Zen isn't something for special occasions, but an everyday path to enlightenment. It makes everything we do, even chores like chopping vegetables or sweeping the floor, feel more meditative and meaningful.

What's more, the benefits of Zen ripple outward from us to the world. When we achieve inner peace, we radiate peace to others. When we understand our interconnectedness with humanity and the cosmos, we're filled with love and compassion for all beings. We do everything in our power to help and not harm them. It's a lovely, satisfying, and very serene way to live.

equanimity

Drama may add spice to life, but it can also drag you down. Better to keep calm and carry on by cultivating equanimity. Such a lovely word, equanimity; it means staying cool and composed even in difficult circumstances. It's moving through life on an even keel, rather than an emotional roller coaster.

I know, that's easier said than done; sometimes we just can't help making a big deal about something. But the worries, tears, and confrontations that ensue are an additional load we don't need to carry. Unchecked, minor incidents can turn into full-blown feuds, and the bad blood can linger indefinitely. With a little equanimity, we can put a damper on these situations from the start, keeping them from spiraling out of control and complicating our lives.

First, don't be overly sensitive. When you take everything personally, you pile on the distress. Instead of letting things ruffle your feathers, let them pass and move on with your life.

Give others the benefit of the doubt. Sometimes a snippy remark is the result of a bad day, not a personal attack. Remember that others are struggling with their own problems, and give them some leeway.

Take time out before you react, and think before you speak. A few minutes or deep breaths can avert a potential meltdown. Ill-considered words make the situation heavier, so keep things light by holding your tongue.

Act with kindness, and choose compassion over confrontation. A gentle word or helpful act can turn almost any situation into a positive one. At the very least, your thoughtful gesture might surprise and disarm your antagonizer.

Keep things in perspective. Ninety-nine percent of the time, the crisis du jour is not the end of the world. Consider whether you'll even remember it next week, next month, or next year.

Don't hold grudges or vow revenge. Even if someone wronged you, negative emotions just add salt to the wound and hurt you more than the object of your ire. Forgive and forget instead of stewing and plotting.

And by all means, don't go looking for drama. Sometimes —perhaps to avoid facing our own issues—we interfere in other people's affairs. But your life will be far lighter if you mind your own business and stay out of everyone else's. If they want your help, they'll ask for it.

In a culture that thrives on conflict and sensationalism, equanimity is something of a lost art. We're often quick to fire back at critics or air our grievances, particularly when we're behind a keyboard. Unfortunately, such interactions can come back to haunt us. Instead, we need to press our pause button; the more imperturbable we are, the lighter and happier we'll be.

Having equanimity doesn't mean being an ice queen or bottling up your emotions. It means exercising some self-control so you can defuse a situation, preventing headaches, heartaches, heaviness, and grief. It's refusing to take the bait, and instead responding with grace and composure.

When tensions are rising, think "Lightly" before you react. Do your best to maintain your poise, even if it means biting your tongue, logging off, or walking away. With practice, you'll develop the strength of mind to remain transcendently calm and rise above the fray.

- Are you currently involved in unnecessary drama (a workplace rivalry, a contentious discussion board)? Make a plan to extract yourself from the situation, and avoid others like it in the future.

- Think about the type of scenarios in which you overreact, and how you might handle the next occurrence with more composure.

- Choose an equanimity role model (be it your grandmother or the Dalai Lama). The next time you're on the edge of turmoil, consider how that person would address a similar circumstance.

Let your soul stand
COOL AND COMPOSED
before a million
universes.

WALT WHITMAN

feel lightly

Do you ever feel weighed down by anger, guilt, sadness, fear, or worry? Such emotions can darken our days and dampen our spirits. Sometimes they press so heavily on us, we can barely function.

Here's the good news: You can feel lighter by simply letting them go. When you purge your physical clutter—the clothes, gadgets, and tchotchkes you don't need—you practice non-attachment. You identify them, evaluate their usefulness, and decide if they belong in your life. For example, this is a pot I never use; this is a dress I rarely wear. Instead of holding tight to these objects, you open your hands and let them go.

You can practice the same non-attachment with your inner clutter—all those negative emotions bringing you down. When your blood starts to boil on your morning commute, stop and think: *This is anger that I'm stuck in traffic. It's not helping me address the situation, but making me tense and jeopardizing my driving. I'll release this feeling and breathe more easily.*

Or when your coworker gets the promotion you wanted: *This is jealousy I feel over my colleague's success. It's not helping me accomplish anything, but making me miserable and less productive. I'll release this emotion and assess my options.*

Instead of holding tight to these feelings, you open your heart and let them go.

Just like your possessions, your emotions aren't part of you. They're simply feelings that arise temporarily in response to a situation. When you feel lightly, you become aware of them and experience them, sometimes deeply. But instead of clinging to them, you let them naturally fall away.

It's like watching your emotions on a movie screen. You recognize them when they appear: Here's Guilt making an entrance; there's Worry in the background. But instead of freezing the frame or replaying them over and over, you let them roll by and then exit the scene.

When you feel lightly, you don't insulate yourself from negative emotions, you simply become mindful of them. You greet them, deal with them, and part ways instead of fixating on them.

To feel lightly is to feel fluidly. You open the channels of your heart so that instead of getting stuck, your emotions ebb and flow.

Of course, some feelings are more difficult to release than others. For those that are long-standing or deeply entrenched, further measures may be in order.

One strategy is to talk about them. Confiding in a trusted friend or professional therapist can be a powerful form of release. Another is to journal about them. Write exactly how you feel, why you feel that way, and what it would take to move on. When you articulate your emotions, you see them more objectively and can separate from them more easily.

Shining a light on troublesome feelings is the first step toward letting them go. Sharing them, whether on paper or with another person, offloads some of the burden, bringing an immediate sense of lightness and relief.

The ancient Egyptians believed that after you died, your heart was weighed; if it was light as a feather, your soul was granted eternal bliss in the afterlife. I believe that if we can be a little more lighthearted now, we can find bliss right here on earth.

    ❁ Identify any emotion that weighs on your heart, and how it came to be. (Example: I feel guilty over a broken promise; I feel anger about a past event.)

    ❁ Determine what steps you can take to let this feeling go (like apologizing, making amends, or seeking therapy).

    ❁ Practice recognizing and releasing your feelings on a daily basis. ("Hi there, Fear. Thanks for stopping by, but I've got this—you can go now.")

speak lightly

Words are powerful. They can inspire, they can instigate, they can soothe, they can sting, they can heal, they can harm.

Therefore, we should think carefully about our words before we voice them. Careless or hurtful remarks don't always dissipate with the conversation; they can linger, adding significant weight and complication to our lives. No matter how much you regret it, you can't unsay something you shouldn't have said.

At other times, our words aren't harmful; we simply say too much. We feel the need to fill the silence and end up telling a stranger our life story, rambling on about something insignificant, or inadvertently dominating the conversation. If we're too talkative, we risk others losing interest in, or giving little import to, what we have to say.

We can avoid these problems by speaking lightly: choosing our words, and the occasions on which we speak, with the utmost care.

An old Sufi proverb recommends that before we say something, we ask the following: Is it true? Is it kind? Is it necessary?

Is it true? First and foremost, avoid gossip. Not only might rumors be false, it's rude to talk behind someone's back. Refrain from exaggerations as well. Don't tell your partner he "never helps around the house" when he forgot to unload the dishwasher, or your child that she'll be flipping burgers if she fails her math test. And always verify the accuracy of information you pass along. Just because you heard it through the grapevine or read it on the Internet doesn't mean it's true.

Is it kind? We all learned as children if you don't have something nice to say, don't say anything at all. Nothing good ever comes of hateful or harmful speech. Hold your criticisms, corrections, and comments unless they can be framed in a helpful manner. And certainly don't be combative or confrontational with your words; issues are resolved more expediently with gentle, diplomatic language.

Is it necessary? Just because we have an opinion on everything doesn't mean the world needs to hear it. Before you grouse about work to your partner, get on your soapbox at a cocktail party, or talk your sister's ear off about the latest celebrity scandal, pause and consider if what you're about to say really needs to be said. Save your words for when you have something valuable to add to the conversation.

Remember, some things are better left unsaid. Don't be the person voicing their frustration in a long post office line (and making everyone else uncomfortable). And before you rant about your rough day at the dinner table, consider whether your family might prefer a more peaceful time together.

Speak lightly not only in conversation, but also on the Internet. Use the aforementioned filters when tweeting, commenting on blogs, or participating in online forums. Don't let anonymity tempt you to be less courteous and judicious than you might be in person, and remember that whatever you write might be archived forever.

When we speak lightly, a wonderful thing happens: We can actually listen. Instead of voicing our own thoughts and opinions, we hear someone else's. We gain new knowledge, a new perspective, a new appreciation for the other side of an issue. We become better parents, partners, and participants in our community, lightening life not only for ourselves but for everyone around us.

- Become more aware of your conversations and pinpoint any trouble spots. Do you tend to interrupt, complain, criticize, or pontificate?

- Think of some specific ways you can speak more lightly (for instance, stop gossiping with your coworkers or nagging your partner).

- The next time you comment on someone's blog or participate in a discussion forum, choose your words carefully. Don't write anything you wouldn't say to them in person.

No sky is heavy
if the heart be
LIGHT.

CHARLES CHURCHILL

walk

If you want to be lighter in body, mind, and spirit, take up a walking practice. It's the easiest thing in the world to do: Simply step out your front door, and put one foot in front of the other.

Why is walking so magical?

Walking immediately lifts your mood. The mere act of getting out of your chair, and into the fresh air, does wonders for your well-being.

Walking is a respite from your busy day. Resist the urge to multitask; in other words, don't take that business call while you're wandering about. Walk away from your worries, figuratively and literally, for at least a short while. You'll come back feeling refreshed and rebalanced.

Walking expands your view and changes your perspective. The problems that loomed large in your home or office seem smaller when you're out in the wide world. If you're in an urban area, your troubles may pale in comparison to others you see. If you're in nature, the grandeur of the scenery may render them insignificant.

Walking grounds you. The process of touching foot to earth, foot to earth, brings you out of the virtual world and into the real one. Gazing into the distance, instead of at a screen, helps you refocus on what it means to be human.

Walking clears your mind, and can be a wonderful form of meditation. Leave the headphones and smartphone at home, and focus on your stride and breath. Set a relaxed pace, and let the rhythmic motion still your thoughts.

Walking connects you to people. Social interaction, even if it's just a brief chat with a neighbor or a smile at a stranger, lifts your spirits. It strengthens your bond with your neighborhood and your community, reminding you that you're not alone in the world.

Walking connects you to nature. Research shows that strolling in greenspaces can reduce stress, anxiety, and depression. Time spent among trees, grass, flowers, and water has a restorative effect on your body and brain. Perhaps it reminds us of a more primal, Elysian state before we had to worry about overdue bills and overflowing inboxes.

Walking lightens your body. It's physical exercise that burns calories, meaning that the more you do it, the less weight you'll carry around. That makes for a healthier, happier, more energetic you.

Walking lightens your burdens. When you're out on foot, you can carry only so much. Channel your inner wandering monk, free of earthly possessions and cares. Savor that freedom, and contemplate ways you can bring more of it into your life.

Walk without a destination and enjoy the journey. Imagine that with each step, you're shedding a care, a worry, a burden, a fear. For a few minutes, forget about your house full of possessions and your schedule full of commitments, and picture yourself as one with the world—the earth rising up through your feet, the air flowing through your body, the sun (or rain) soaking into your skin. You'll return home lighter for the experience.

- ↖ Go for a walk every day, rain or shine, even if it's just around the block. Don't concern yourself with counting steps or miles; it's not a competitive pursuit, it's a contemplative one.

- ↖ When you're walking, focus on the present moment. Instead of getting lost in thought, drink in your surroundings. Be fully aware of what you see, hear, smell, and feel. Appreciate the beauty of every tree, flower, or person you encounter.

- ↖ If possible, run errands on foot. You'll be much more mindful of what you buy when you have to carry it home. When you relocate, consider walkability in your housing search.

quantum physics

Mass is a fundamental property in classic Newtonian physics—the kind that deals with the movement of planets or a rock rolling down a hill. It's a science built on weight and gravity that nicely describes and predicts the behavior of the ordinary objects we observe around us.

However, Newton's concept of solid building blocks breaks down when we look beyond the visible, to the tiny world of subatomic particles or the grand scale of the cosmos. That's where quantum physics comes into play, and paints a much more ethereal picture of matter.

What we (and everything else) are ultimately made of aren't solid bits, but rather a field of quantum fluctuations—an evanescent dance of particles flickering in and out of existence. That's quite a reality check.

What's more, today's Standard Model of physics rests on the existence of the Higgs boson (or "God particle"), whose quantum field gives other particles their mass. In 2012, this elusive particle was detected with the Large Hadron Collider, to great celebration in the scientific community. Yet what really surprised physicists and still leaves them perplexed: that instead of the heavy particle they expected, the Higgs boson they found was *so very light*.

It'll be fascinating to see what quantum physics reveals about the true nature of reality. But perhaps it already gives us a scientific basis for why it feels so good, so natural to cast off our excess weight. For when we look deeply at the essence of being, what we find is lightness.

let go of your ego

One of the heaviest things you carry around is your own ego.

Your ego is your "I." It's what you generally think of as your "self," as distinct from the world and other people.

Your ego is like a funnel into which you pour all those things that make up your identity: wife, mother, sister, daughter, lawyer, cyclist, member of an ethnic group, religion, or organization. It's how you describe yourself to yourself and the world.

Your ego is supremely concerned about "me." It's the part that feels offended (*he said what about me?*), proud (*she's not as stylish as me*), jealous (*he's richer than me*), worried (*will they fire me?*), and insecure (*nobody likes me*).

It's that little voice in your head that keeps up a running monologue all day, making judgments (*I like this, I don't like that*), voicing anxieties (*I'm not good enough, smart enough, pretty enough*), and generally driving you crazy.

The problem: Your ego is not your true self. It's just a psychological construct that comes with a lot of baggage, and you'd be much lighter without it.

Your ego has no permanence. If you weren't a wife, mother, lawyer, or member of a certain religion, you'd still be you. If you had different likes, dislikes, opinions, or political party affiliations, you'd still be you. If you changed your mind about a long-held belief, you'd still be you.

Even your body—the "I" you see in the mirror—isn't permanent. Your cells and tissues undergo constant renewal and replacement; for a large part, the molecules and microbes that make up your physical body are different than those you had last week, last month, last year. What's more, you're made of and dependent upon your surroundings—earth, air, water, sunlight—for your very survival.

Both physically and psychologically, you're in a constant state of flux. You're more of an experience, a coming together of favorable elements, than a fixed entity.

What a wonderful opportunity to lighten up! You can ditch the burden of your ego without losing your true self. In fact, letting go of your ego helps you find your true self. Once you quiet that voice in your head, you'll find an amazing sense of peace and calm. Your true self doesn't need to prove anything to anybody. It simply is.

When you embrace your true self, you're enraptured by a beautiful sunrise, without having to share it on social media to prove you're a nature lover.

When you embrace your true self, you don't fall to pieces if you lose your job, your marriage, or your membership in a particular group, because you're not dependent on those labels for your self-worth.

When you embrace your true self, you don't take things personally. You lose that "me versus the world" mentality, because you realize you're inseparable from everything around you.

Your ego thinks you're an island, when in reality we're all

waves on the same ocean of consciousness. When you disconnect from your ego, you reconnect to the universe.

So feel free to let go of your ego and everything you've piled upon it. Release all those burdens that come with defining, projecting, and protecting your sense of self; they serve no real purpose other than to weigh you down.

Your ego is the caterpillar, encasing itself in a secure but cumbersome chrysalis. When you embrace your true self, you shed that earthbound skin and soar with the lightness and freedom of a butterfly.

- As you go about your day, be aware of the chatter in your head. Address it as you would a friend — "Hello Ego, you're quite talkative today." Maybe ask it to quiet down for a bit.

- When you're weighed down with worries over your looks, your job title, your social status, remind yourself you're so much more than that. You're a wondrous, ethereal being who's presently walking this earth.

- When you feel lonely or isolated, remember you are one with everyone on this planet, everything in the universe. Reach out to someone, friend or stranger, online or off, to make a connection. Take comfort that by your very nature, you are never alone.

be fluid

If life were a calm and placid pool, we could navigate its waters with ease. Instead, it's more like a flowing river, ever moving and ever changing. Imagine trying to stand against the current; you may hang in there for a bit, but eventually you'll be exhausted and pulled helplessly along (or worse yet, under).

When we resist change in our lives, we feel the same pressure. Whether we're clinging to an idea, a relationship, or a situation, our efforts to fix them in time leave us frustrated and fatigued. When we're finally forced to adjust, it's all the more difficult.

When we live lightly, we realize that nothing is permanent. The tides of change are beyond our control, so instead of blocking the flow, we go with it. That way, we have the chance to adapt naturally and gracefully to new situations, instead of being dragged along. Being fluid does not mean being weak or passive. It means understanding that change is natural and inevitable, and accepting rather than resisting it.

People change. When we're fluid, we enjoy watching our kids grow up instead of wishing they'd stay little. We welcome our partner's new interests and ideas even if they're not the same as our own. We let our friendships evolve with time instead of rooting them in the past.

Places change. When we're fluid, we accept that our city, our town, our street won't be the same as when we grew up or when we moved in. We welcome new people and ideas into our community. Conversely, when opportunities arise, we don't feel stuck in place; we go where we need to be to live life to the fullest.

Plans change. When we're fluid, we realize that our days, our relationships, our careers may not unfold as expected. Instead of despairing when life derails our plans — whether it's a missed flight or a job layoff — we adapt to the situation and trust that things will work out for the best.

Circumstances change. When we're fluid, we know that "this too shall pass." We know that a bad situation won't last forever, and we look toward the future with hope rather than fixating on our troubles. Conversely, we're grateful for our current blessings and don't take anything for granted.

We change. When we're fluid, we don't agonize over those wrinkles, those laugh lines, and those first gray hairs. We age gracefully instead of trying to turn back time. We're open-minded rather than fixed in our thinking. Instead of holding on to who we were, we welcome the person we're becoming.

When we're fluid, we let people, possessions, and ideas move into and out of our lives without becoming attached to them. We go through life with open arms, ready to welcome and to release. Instead of being rigid in our views and set in our ways, we greet change with flexibility, curiosity, and a sense of humor.

We recognize that the universe will unfold of its own beautiful accord, so we might as well relax and enjoy our part in it. That way, rather than sink under the weight of our burdens, we can float lightly and tranquilly along the river of life.

- In what area of life are you resisting change (your body, your family, your workplace)? What might happen if you go with the flow instead of fighting it?

- If you have strongly held beliefs, read or listen to alternate viewpoints. Hearing different perspectives can make you more flexible and understanding in your dealings with others.

- Do you feel the need to plan everything down to the last detail? Whether it's your weekend, vacation, or long-term career plan, try taking each day as it comes. You may be surprised and delighted by what transpires.

The perfection
of human nature is
SWEETNESS
and
LIGHT.

MATTHEW ARNOLD

be kind

In my daughter's kindergarten, the children were assigned a job each day from a list of tasks (Door Holder, Fish Feeder, Gardener, etc.). My favorite was Kindness Reporter—a role that involved noticing others' kind acts and sharing them with the class. How brilliant is that? I wish my news feed had such a report!

Being kind is one of the simplest and most effective ways to achieve lightness of spirit. Studies have shown that when we do nice things for other people, we become happier ourselves. Yes, it's that easy. And it doesn't have to be a grand gesture or a big donation. Simply extending a good deed, caring word, or thoughtful act toward someone else can make your spirits soar.

For best results, be kind to everyone, everywhere, all the time. Kindness comes easily when we're in a good mood, and we generally have no problem being benevolent toward our loved ones. We have to make a greater effort when we're feeling tired, dejected, or disgruntled ourselves, or when the person we're facing is causing us grief. But that's when a little act of kindness can have the most transformative effect.

When your child throws a tantrum, wets the bed, or wakes you up at 3:30 a.m., respond with kindness.

When your partner snaps at you after a hard day at work, respond with kindness.

When your grumpy neighbor knocks on your door to complain, respond with kindness.

When a frazzled server spills your coffee or brings you the wrong order, respond with kindness.

When someone makes a nasty comment about you on social media, respond with kindness.

These situations could ruin your day (and then some) if you get annoyed, lash out, or retaliate. Worse yet, they could create additional, long-lasting burdens for you to carry, like bad blood, negative feelings, and troubled relationships. Kindness, on the other hand, immediately lightens the encounter, leaving both parties relieved of trouble and stress.

Of course, you don't have to wait for an opportunity to do good. Consider performing random acts of kindness for strangers; it'll brighten both your day and someone else's. Some ideas: compliment people on the street, leave friendly notes in public places, put dollar bills in library books, buy coffee for the next person in line, write a nice comment on someone's blog, take flowers to a senior center.

You can take your kindness practice beyond the individual level, and let it inform your consumer choices as well. Don't purchase clothes from brands that use sweatshops, cosmetics from companies that harm animals, or goods that pollute the planet. You'll extend kindness to the people, animals, and environment affected by these practices, and lighten burdens on a worldwide scale.

And by all means, be kind to yourself. When you look in the mirror each morning, give yourself a smile and some words of encouragement. Take some time out for self-care: Make sure you get the rest, exercise, and nourishment you need. When you mess up, respond with kindness. Forgive yourself and resolve to do better next time. A little self-love can really lift your spirits.

What's more, kindness has a wonderful ripple effect. The feel-good factor is so high that the giver's inclined to do more, and the receiver's inclined to pay it forward. Thus, one simple act can have exponential results, spreading joy, goodwill, and lightness far and wide.

- Perform at least one act of kindness each day. It can be as simple as smiling at a stranger or yielding to another motorist. How does it make you feel?

- Is there someone with whom you don't get along? Henceforth, be genuinely kind in your interaction with them, regardless of how they respond.

- Notice others' good deeds and be a Kindness Reporter. Share these heartwarming stories with your spouse, your children, or online.

be still

To live lightly is to live mindfully—in other words, to be fully aware in the present moment. When we're not dwelling on the past or worrying about the future, much weight is lifted from our shoulders.

How can we develop such mindfulness? By meditating. When we meditate, we practice focusing our attention on the here and now.

Don't be intimidated by notions of emptying your mind or reaching a blissed-out, spiritual state. That can certainly happen with time and practice; but to start, just find a few minutes each day to be still. Choose a time and place where you won't be disturbed. Then sit up straight in a comfortable position (either in a chair or on the ground), close your eyes, and relax. As you sit, focus on the sensation of breathing: in breath, out breath, in breath, out breath. Nothing fancy, nothing complicated—just breathe naturally.

When thoughts arise (and they most certainly will), don't push them aside. Simply notice them without judging or clinging to them, then let them float away like drifting clouds. Refocus on your breath, and when the next thought arises, do the same.

If you'd like, you can listen to a guided meditation. When you're starting out, it can be helpful to have a trained practitioner lead you step-by-step along the path to awareness.

You'll pick up skills and techniques you can use on your own.

Most important, remember that in meditation, there is no goal. You don't have to worry about accomplishing or achieving anything. All you have to do is *just be* in the present moment.

Meditation is a wonderful way to practice mindfulness because you're sitting still without distractions. It's easier to reach a state of inner calm when you're not surrounded by children, coworkers, ringing phones, and myriad other demands for your attention.

That said, 99 percent of our lives is spent surrounded by children, coworkers, ringing phones, and myriad other demands. So what good is meditation if it lightens up only a tiny fraction of our day?

Believe it or not, experiencing a state of mindfulness for even a short time has significant benefits. Meditation has favorable effects on your body and brain — like lowering blood pressure, heart rate, stress, and anxiety — that last beyond the actual sitting. But ideally, meditation helps us train our brain for mindfulness, so that we can more easily achieve this state *in any situation*: while we're cooking dinner, riding the train, attending a meeting, and all the other things we do on a daily basis. With practice, we can bring that wonderful inner lightness we experience in meditation into our everyday lives.

In Buddhism, meditation is the means to enlightenment, a spiritual state of perfect wisdom in which desire and suffering cease. We, too, can aspire to our own "enlightenment." Freeing our mind of its burdens, we can, at least for a time, feel absolutely weightless.

↗ Give meditation a try, without concern about "doing it right." For a few minutes, simply sit in a chair, be still, and focus on the present moment. That's not so hard, is it?

↗ Make meditation a daily practice, like brushing your teeth. Start with just five minutes a day, and slowly expand the time as desired.

↗ Practice mindfulness in the midst of activity. Be still at the office, on the subway, in line at the coffee shop. No matter what chaos surrounds you, imagine yourself an oasis of calm.